T0063082

Walking

in

Instructions

....

THE WALK OF POWER

Pastor Erick Maosa

WESTBOW°
PRESS
A DIVISION OF THOMAS NELSON
& ZONDERVAN

Scripture taken from the King James Version of the Bible.

All emphasis added to Scripture are the author's.

WestBow Press books may be ordered through booksellers or by contacting:

WestBow Press
A Division of Thomas Nelson & Zondervan
1663 Liberty Drive
Bloomington, IN 47403
www.westbowpress.com
1 (866) 928-1240

ISBN: 978-1-4908-4605-7 (sc)

Library of Congress Control Number: 2014913244

Printed in the United States of America.

WestBow Press rev. date: 09/12/2014

CONTENTS

How do we acquire instructions?

Proverbs 13:18
Poverty and shame shall be to him
that <u>refuseth instruction</u>:
but he that <u>regardeth reproof</u>
shall be honoured.

Dedication

To my dear and loving family

especially my loving parents Pastor Thomas and Jane Maosa.
My brothers, sisters and Lovely niece& nephew

Appreciation

I acknowledge the Mighty grace of the Holy Spirit,
without whom I can do nothing.

Special acknowledgement to my Bishop, Apostle Musili and his lovely family,
the Youth at Around the Globe Deliverance Ministry. Bishop Shadrack
Gona & family for their support in the initial years of my ministry.

Thanks to Pastor Wilson Sowa and his family, Pastor
Ikonze, Bishop Zakaria (Tz) and Pastor Ntepa (Tz).

God bless you all abundantly.

INTRODUCTION

It is every Christian's hope and desire to witness the presence and the power of God in his or her life just as it is written within the Bible. A lot of keys have been delved into i.e. prayer, fasting, sowing etc which aren't wrong. Nevertheless, there has been a minimal experience of the raw power of God in the lives of so many prayer warriors all around the world and over the ages. There is the silent, most overlooked yet powerful key of obedience is yet to be looked into exhaustively.

Obedience to instructions is the bedrock of all the other keys or steps that you may have to engage yourself in. the nature of instructions, the importance of receiving them, following them and also how to receive them is paramount to the exercising of the power of God effectively in our lives.

There is a need for you to take a journey, pouring through the pages of this book and after doing so, I am sure that you will be ready to experience the Almighty power of God in your life.

1. OUR RELATIONSHIP WITH POWER

1 Chronicles 29:11 Thine, O LORD, is the greatness, and the
power, and the glory, and the victory, and the majesty: for
all that is in the heaven and in the earth is thine; thine is the
kingdom, O LORD, and thou art exalted as head above all.

All through existence, the aspect of knowledge has been the one major aspect that is and has been used to set people apart. Knowledge has been and is still explained in various ways or levels of understanding, it can simply be likened to the sharpening of an axe while ignorance, to a blunting of an axe. Obviously, the sharper the axe used is, the more efficient the user is all the while experiencing less strain. This will be opposite when using a blunt axe.

Allow me to inform you about our relationship with power, basing on the understanding that; power is simply one's ability or capacity to influence anything he or she desires, needs or is required to influence. It is wise to first understand that there are two primary kinds of power but both of them are subject to the same Lord, regardless of their channels of application. I use the term primary, due to the fact that all the other kinds of power that we encounter in life are offshoots of these. These are; the earthly *(human based)* power and the heavenly *(spiritual)* power. Earthly power is the kind that is a product of or is subject to man's logic or understanding. It can be developed and applied through normal, human mechanics.

This kind is the power that is normally found within governing bodies and documents like Constitutions of various States, Countries or generally, all civilized societies. It is totally subject to man, for man has delegated authority from God to handle such. It sprouts from the platform of man's thinking ability. We should further note that man may not acknowledge that this power has been delegated to him by a supreme being and this why some say there is no God or follow the social based schools of thought. Let us choose for ourselves how we shall manage ourselves.

Sadly, we are in a world that is growing increasingly rebellious all the more day by day. Even those who were believers at the beginning of their Christian life are today gradually losing faith. This kind is evidenced through how people exercise their wills or the choices that a person makes. These choices on most occasions, are at a personal level like; "*I don't feel like coming with you,*" "*what I do with my car is my own business so back off!*" or "*mum, am now a grown up so I can make my own decisions.*" It can also be witnessed through the more general matters like political office setups where the office-holders' powers are controlled. Ever heard of jurisdictions of mandates?

Due to the already corrupted nature of man and due to it being fanned by the devil; mankind is by the hour, enforcing wickedness in the world just because he has the earthly power to do so. The power to make his own decisions causes him to forget that he exists, not by his own power, but by the hand of his Creator. He fails to understand and appreciate the hand of the Almighty God that formed him. Civil liberties and the ever increasing power of choice are derailing societies today. God is in control by virtue of creating the man in the society but not by the man's recognition of Him as Sovereign.

The other kind of power, as I mentioned earlier, is the heavenly or spiritual power. This power isn't man-dependant though it is or can be wielded by man. Its rules are not based on the logic or limited understanding of men. It is based on the supremacy of the spiritual over the physical. I believe that I should note herein, the actual fact, that there are two planes of existence; the spiritual and the physical. This is regardless of what many may choose to believe. Some do believe that there is no spiritual existence hence they choose to name the spiritual as the "subconscious". We must understand that disbelieving the existence of something doesn't mean it doesn't exist. What exists does exist and that which doesn't exist simply doesn't.

Spiritual power indeed is superior to the earthly kind of power. In some experiences, through spiritual power, people have negatively influenced the earthly power, putting many people or sections of creation under yokes or various types of snares. This is further evidenced when the senior leaders of the people seek the intervention of spiritual-power wielders to help them control earthly power. We see a lot of this in Africa particularly during the election periods.

There are many scenarios where spiritual power clashes with earthly power. I must reiterate herein that, all power belongs to God. A case example, in the Bible, in which the heavenly and earthly powers clashed, is when Abraham met with Abimelech, the king of Gerar. Herein, Abimelech the king used his earthly power which Abraham feared, to take Abraham's wife, Sarah, from him. This was so till God, through heavenly power, intervened. We notice that Abraham's wife dwelt with Abimelech just because he was the king and also that Abraham couldn't do anything concerning that but wait on God.

We realize, that though Abraham and Abimelech we normal men, their power bases were totally different. Abimelech's position granted him, as ruler over that region, earthly power over Abraham which he didn't hesitate to apply. However, Abraham exercised spiritual power over the king due to his faith in the Almighty God. God is Spirit and He is the one who formed all things; we are also spirit as a result of being born again, thus, we also have the required access to heavenly power for our use. This isn't only due to faith, but also upon the platform of being Abraham's seed.

This is also accomplished through praying to our God, in order for Him to influence the earthly power issues that we face. It is written for us to understand, that through faith in God, the people of God influenced and subdued nations (*Hebrews 11:33*). Let's now use the Abraham and Abimelech example in this study;

Genesis 20:2-3 And Abraham said of Sarah his wife, She is my sister: and Abimelech king of Gerar sent, and took Sarah. But God came to Abimelech in a dream by night, and said to him, Behold, thou art but a dead man, for the woman which thou hast taken; for she is a man's wife.

The above duo of verses shows us how both kinds of power came into play at the same time. It is a sort of clash of powers. It will also prove that, though a man is a wielder of power (*earthly*), regardless of how much he wields, he is will be subject to the man who wields heavenly (*spiritual*) power. The Bible instructs us that, though we are from above and not below, we are required to respect earthly authority so that we may have peace.

This however, doesn't necessarily mean that the earthly power holders will always respect our source of authority though they are inevitably subject to it, *Genesis 20:11 And Abraham said, Because I thought, Surely the fear of God is not in this place; and they will slay me for my wife's sake.* It is for the sake of peace that we pray for them. Prayer for them actually is the process through which God will influence them to act in our favour.

We, believers (*spiritual power wielders*), are the ones to pray for the earthly power holders. We get to understand this task through the life of Daniel, the prophet. He changed an enacted law through prayer. He was able to achieve this feat by basing on the fact that we are Christ's ambassadors on earth. Therefore, we are able enforce God's will, here on earth, as it is in heaven. In heaven, there is no compromise; it is either God's way or none at all. We can learn this from looking at the example of Jacob and his uncle Laban when confronting each other.

> *Genesis 31:29 It is in the power of my hand to do you hurt: but the God of your father spake unto me yesternight, saying, Take thou heed that thou speak not to Jacob either good or bad.*

When talking about the possession and wielding of power, there is also the question of how strong one is in either or both power systems. The president, of a super-power nation, can influence the earthly power system of a weaker Nation. A strong spiritual leader will ultimately influence earthly power whereas one who is weak in spiritual power can be influenced by one with earthly power. This was the case for the seeds which were choked by the desires of the things of the world shown through earthly objects in the parable of *the sower*.

Though I am a believing Christian, I have come to acknowledge this; that the other religions, besides Christianity, do actually have spiritual power too though it isn't obtained through faith in Christ Jesus. They also do influence most of the earthly systems around the world. This is the very bedrock of spiritual warfare; a war fought not by earthly power but by heavenly power, on the earth. The earth is a battle ground just the heavens (*spiritual realms; these aren't the Heaven of heavens where God dwells*) are.

This is why it is extremely wise, for us Christians, to make a distinction between our God and the other people's or religions' gods. They may seem to be powerful and influential, but only our God is God. I believe that you, the reader, by now have a relatively good understanding of how we relate with power, in the heavenly aspect and in the earthly aspect too.

Furthermore, we must be careful, concerning what we are taught about power, whether within the church circles or outside; for it is this knowledge that enables one, to either, successfully wield heavenly power on earth or be in constant defeat. Knowledge in itself is acquired and is easily transferred from one to another. The kind of knowledge am talking about is operative knowledge (*effective; producing a desired effect*) in your life. The knowledge, of God, that functions and by which you live your life. What one has acquired becomes the foundation of another's knowledge.

However, God may, at times, decide to directly equip you by His Spirit as He did for Moses and Abraham. Regardless of how we acquired it, we all need each other in order to learn and become effective. This makes it all the more paramount to gain a good understanding through rightly dividing the Word of God. The poor knowledge that may be possessed by one, won't necessarily remain a personal matter but can also influence another's failure. This isn't specifically about false teachers, it also concerns people that were taught the wrong thing, it became a doctrine to them and now they are also teaching the same thing. For example, we are taught and also sing that "pass me not oh gentle Saviour"; it sounds good but it is wrong. Jesus dwells in our hearts through faith *Ephesians 3:17* and we in Him in the heavenly places *Ephesians 2:6*. It isn't sensible for the one you dwell in to pass you by now, is it?

If I believe that Jesus is weak and teach people so, those who listen to me and believe in my teaching will grow and face the world knowing that Jesus is limited. Their failure will be an extension of my poor knowledge.

Some people have grown up knowing that God doesn't give birth or get born. That Jesus cannot be His Son for that will purport that He go married. This is what they were taught and the result of this is refusing Jesus' status as the only way to the Father.

Acquired knowledge about power is extremely sensitive for it can either serve to build or to destroy you. You have and need to be taught right. Let us take note of these verses herein, *2 Timothy 2:15-18 Study to shew thyself approved unto God, a workman that needeth not to be ashamed, rightly dividing the word of truth. But shun profane and vain babblings: for they will increase unto more ungodliness. And their word will eat as doth a canker: of whom is Hymenaeus and Philetus; Who concerning the truth have erred, saying that the resurrection is past already; and overthrow the faith of some.* You do realize that Apostle Paul is directing Timothy that he must have the capacity to rightly divide the Word of God for he will be handling God's people living within a pagan society.

Pagan doesn't mean powerless; it simply means believers in other gods but not our God. The other teachers, who did it wrongly, led others to lose faith. I was raised up in church believing that the apostles and prophets in the Bible were more special than I. this changed when I gained the right knowledge of the Word of God.

Concerning our relationship with power, there is a good reason why God promised us shepherds that will teach us in accordance with God's knowledge and understanding. Wrong knowledge may as well be as bad as or worse than ignorance. People will know your God based on what you know about Him through exercising that knowledge. May they praise your God because the right knowledge that you have about Him. You cannot have a good relationship with power when you are ignorant or have the wrong information about it.

Jeremiah 3:15 And I will give you pastors according to mine heart, which shall feed you with knowledge and understanding.

The common teaching within many sections of the church, about heavenly power is that, it belongs only to God, the Biblically listed Apostles and a few generals of faith in the world who had a special encounter with God. Many Christians are very cold, towards the subject of power, with some terming it as arrogance or disregarding God and are afraid of venturing into this topic of power citing various reasons. Many believe that because Jesus Christ made a show of all powers of darkness at the Cross, there is no need ask to possess power. I believe, that many have little knowledge hence are of little faith and think that God may leave them hanging in front of people or because of many other irrelevant reasons.

Power is always practical, so when talking about it, you will also be needed to demonstrate it and this is what's most challenging for many.

As I grew up some more in Salvation, after much meditation and the interaction with various heavily anointed ministers of the Gospel; I realized, some wrong information that had been and may still be taught unto many today hence the mediocre results we see in Christians' lives today. Many custodians of the Truth teach what they think is right but not that which is true according to the Holy Spirit's revelation. It is very possible to preach the Gospel without power. Some use motivational talents or artistic creativity. However, at the end of it all, the devil might win in the lives of many that follow these.

This is the issue of preaching about a Mighty God but experiencing nothing of His mightiness in your life. There is a reason why Jesus Christ came from the wilderness, full of the Spirit and with power. He was compared to the other teachers and this is what was stated in *Mark 1:22 And they were astonished at his doctrine: for he taught them as one that had authority, and not as the scribes.* A similar verse is in *Luke 4:36 And they were all amazed, and spake among themselves, saying, What a word is this! for with authority and power he commandeth the unclean spirits, and they come out.*

This is also why we struggle with each other in cheap doctrinal wars like whether demons exist, necessity of deliverance after Salvation, whether a Christian can be oppressed by demons and even on how to baptise. This is the fundamental point; that the Word of God without power, is useless and power must be demonstrated. If the church won't demonstrate it through whichever available avenue e.g. healings, deliverance, prophesies etc, satan will keep outwitting us; swaying the world to himself. It's not about speaking or teaching in political correctness, but simply about the truth.

2 Corinthians 2:11 Lest Satan should get an advantage
of us: for we are not ignorant of his devices.

1 Corinthians 2:4-5 And my speech and my preaching was not
with enticing words of man's wisdom, but in demonstration
of the Spirit and of power: That your faith should not stand
in the wisdom of men, but in the power of God.

What you have been taught, is exactly what will constitute your very being; no more no less. Your knowledge will determine how your perception of all things is, particularly when it comes to functioning beyond the conventional. The knowledge you feed yourself on is what will dictate the functioning status of your power. As we are enlightened through *1 Corinthians 2:4-5*, there are many who have rested their faith on human wisdom thus ending up being tossed to and fro by the devil.

In the next chapter, we shall be going through the various aspects of power, so that there can be better understanding of what power is and what its role is in our lives, as believers in Christ Jesus. On focusing on our relationship with power, we must have the primary knowledge that we do have power or rather full access to it. It is accessed through the name of Christ Jesus not only because we have the Holy Spirit within us, but also because of whom Jesus made us to be in God.

We must also understand which kind of power this is, that we have access to; *Ephesians 1:19-21 And what is the exceeding greatness of his power to us-ward who believe, according to the working of his mighty power, Which he wrought in Christ, when he raised him from the dead, and set him at his own right hand in the heavenly places, Far above all principality, and power, and might, and dominion, and every name that is named, not only in this world, but also in that which is to come.*

As we venture into the next chapter, let it be clear, once again, that it's the Almighty power of God which rules over earthly power and not any other kind of power regardless of its source. To us, now, power is a gift given to us by our loving, self-sustaining Father. It wasn't ours before, but now is. It is within our sphere (*control zone*). It shouldn't be unique or as a surprise, but part of our originality now.

2.   INTO POWER

From this point and the rest of this book, we shall dwell mainly on heavenly power and not the earthly power. This book is mainly concerned with heavenly power for the believers in Christ; power that is attained through faith in God through Jesus Christ. This is because, regardless of all things and as they may be or seem to be, it is still the one with heavenly power who will ultimately subjugate it. This is why God, our Father, has given us the duty to influence the world and the heavens through our prayers. Jesus came to do His Father's will, not by the power of men, but by the power of God and this is exactly what He told Pontius Pilate. He let Pilate know that he stood to judge because God had allowed to do so. I want us to look into the power given to us that can make us talk like this and act like Jesus Christ; practically and not theoretically.

It is about us getting to access the power that originates from the Kingdom to which we now belong; so that we can bring the requisite glory to our God. *1 Corinthians 2:15 But he that is spiritual judgeth all things, yet he himself is judged of no man.* A Christian must represent Christ fully and effectively here on earth. It isn't the one with earthly power that will heal a man suffering from HIV/Aids but the one with heavenly power. Demons will not fear any one, even an elected president or the richest one on earth, they will only fear the one who kneels before the Father in the Spirit.

> *Daniel 2:44 And in the days of these kings shall the God of heaven set up a kingdom, which shall never be destroyed: and the kingdom shall not be left to other people, but it shall break in pieces and consume all these kingdoms, and it shall stand for ever.*

There is a base statement about power that I will start with; that power has a nature. Power doesn't just exist, floating amorphously within the atmosphere, so that anyone can just pick it up. Even the air we breathe has its unique nature. Furthermore, I wish to expressly state that I don't have all knowledge of all things of God. There will always be more to learn through revelation from the Holy Spirit. What I have compiled within this book, is the fraction of knowledge that the Holy Spirit has graced me with. May God avail to you more knowledge, so that we can all be effective in the edification of the body of Christ.

The mechanics of power have to be well understood, otherwise, the results will be more of catastrophic instead of productive. We also must understand that power doesn't just belong to "God"; the universally acknowledged deity. It solely belongs to our God; the God of the Christians, Jehovah EL-Shaddai. This is the Father of Our Lord Jesus Christ; the risen King of kings. Other religions do use the title *God* as the acceptable title for a supreme deity as well as their own deities. On our part, it is YAHWEH. What you may call an idol, may be actually referred to as creator by someone else who believes in it as such. It is a must that we distinguish Our God from the others' *(non-believers) God or gods*. We must show distinctive association and affiliation to our God.

Our God made us distinct unto Himself; we are different from other people, belong to Him and are most precious unto Him. We are born of the Spirit through faith in Christ Jesus unlike the others who don't acknowledge His Sonship or His position in the Godhead. Those not born of the Spirit are dead but we are alive. Life can only come into a man through faith in Christ Jesus. When talking about power as a topic you will have to look at it, not merely as a normal man, but as a product of the Giver of power.

1 Peter 2:9 But ye are a chosen generation, a royal priesthood, an holy nation, a peculiar people; that ye should shew forth the praises of him who hath called you out of darkness into his marvellous light:

Isaiah 37:16 O LORD of hosts, God of Israel, that dwellest between the cherubims, thou art the God, <u>even thou alone</u>, of all the kingdoms of the earth: thou hast made heaven and earth.

Some summary aspects of power;

a) Power belongs to Our God

> *Psalms 62:11 God hath spoken once; twice have I*
> *heard this; that power belongeth unto God.*

I did note earlier, that power has a nature. One of the aspects in its nature is that it has an origin. Power didn't just pop into existence but was formed. Many people confuse the Holy Spirit with power thinking that He is the power of God. This is extremely wrong; the Holy Spirit is God and power belongs to Him. From whence did power originate? Who brought it into existence? The answer to the above questions is simple; Our God. It is He who releases power into the various areas of general life, via various modes; through man, animals, objects and general creation. It is our God who, by His own will, releases power to one for this and to another for that, even when it seems as if He isn't in control.

> *Numbers 22:28-30 And the LORD opened the mouth of the ass, and*
> *she said unto Balaam, What have I done unto thee, that thou hast*
> *smitten me these three times? And Balaam said unto the ass, Because*
> *thou hast mocked me: I would there were a sword in mine hand,*
> *for now would I kill thee. And the ass said unto Balaam, Am not I*
> *thine ass, upon which thou hast ridden ever since I was thine unto*
> *this day? was I ever wont to do so unto thee? And he said, Nay.*

All power bows to our God and belongs solely to Him. There isn't, in existence, any partnership between Him with any other concerning power. It doesn't belong to any of the other deities for they are simply; satan and his pawns, tricking people so as to receive worship unto themselves.

> *1 Corinthians 8:4-6 As concerning therefore the eating of those things that are*
> *offered in sacrifice unto idols, we know that an idol is nothing in the world,*
> *and that there is none other God but one. For though there be that are called*
> *gods, whether in heaven or in earth, (as there be gods many, and lords many,)*
> *But to us there is but one God, the Father, of whom are all things, and we*
> *in him; and one Lord Jesus Christ, by whom are all things, and we by him.*

These above verses come in handy when shading more light in this subject at hand; that the devil does bring up various worship systems through which he tries to contend with the Truth. He shall obviously fail and eventually, in our God's timing, be thrown into the lake of eternal fire. I'll be glad to see that ultimate occurrence and rejoice over it with the rest of my brethren in Christ, the saints.

Religions of the world, regardless of how great or holy many of them seem, have been designed by the devil through the power that he received from our God while still an angel. It is now dependent on the saints to deal with him through the knowledge and the power acquired through our God's instructions. Jesus Christ came for us to receive power to dominate his wiles and set others free from his hold. What we have now, is the power to prove that his works were already dealt with by our Lord Jesus Christ on the Cross at Calvary (*Colossians 2:14 and 1 John 3:8*).

> *Daniel 11:32-33 And such as do wickedly against the covenant shall he corrupt by flatteries: but the people <u>that do know their God</u> shall be strong, and do exploits. And they that understand among the people <u>shall instruct many</u>: yet they shall fall by the sword, and by flame, by captivity, and by spoil, many days.*

When facing any challenge, your understanding must always be that whatever that is challenging you is still subject to your God. Don't let your mind be divided on this matter at any time. Whether it is presidential authority, occultic power etc for their progenitors came into existence through Christ Jesus *John 1:3 All things were made by him; and without him was not any thing made that was made* and *Colossians 1:16-17 For by him were all things created, that are in heaven, and that are in earth, visible and invisible, whether they be thrones, or dominions, or principalities, or powers: all things were created by him, and for him: And he is before all things, and by him all things consist.*

b) Power is for all those in Christ Jesus

> *Ephesians 1:19-20 And what is the exceeding greatness of his power to us-ward who believe, according to the working of his mighty*

power, Which he wrought in Christ, when he raised him from the
dead, and set him at his own right hand in the heavenly places,

The issue of who can or should demonstrate power is crucial and has been in extreme contention for a long time. This issue is so contentious such that; if a man of God experiences a few miracles in his ministry, people will either adore him exceedingly or dispute with him believing and arguing that he is using demonic empowerment to mesmerize people *Mathew 12:24 But when the Pharisees heard it, they said, This fellow doth not cast out devils, but by Beelzebub the prince of the devils.* Some servants of God did develop the element of pride, causing them to shipwreck their faith. Many people, including the tongue speaking Christians, do opt shy away from the action of demonstrating power. I have witnessed many men of God get labeled devil worshippers or corrupt because of demonstrating power and using prophetic tools.

They do think to be humility, not to desire to carry out great feats like those mentioned in the Bible. They don't think that they can do more than Apostle Paul or other Biblical greats. It is clear in the Bible that it is God who did these great things through them and can certainly do the same through us for we inherited the same faith. This is because their mindsets are a product of a wrong school of thought. They believe that the Apostles and Prophets of old were exceedingly special, which is obviously a lie from the devil.

We need to remember the advice that Apostle peter gave us concerning the complex teachings that God gave Paul that many who didn't understand tried to corrupt *2 Peter 3:15-16 And account that the longsuffering of our Lord is salvation; even as our beloved brother Paul also according to the wisdom given unto him hath written unto you; As also in all his epistles, speaking in them of these things; in which are some things hard to be understood, which they that are unlearned and unstable wrest, as they do also the other scriptures, unto their own destruction.*

Personally, though this may as well include you too, when growing up within the church precincts. I was convinced that it was just the few people who had met with God under special circumstances that should be looked upon to save us all. Due to this school of thought, I grew up with a limited understanding of the Word of God and even more limited in my spirituality.

I overly revered the Biblical personalities that God used to spread the Word. Worse yet, there are many that have been caused to believe that there are no more miracles; that we are confined to the natural order of things because Jesus Christ did redemptive work at the Cross. That it's okay to be ill, for God knows that you are ill and that you wouldn't have been ill had it not been His will.

This, of course, was total hogwash. You have the power to decree your healing and that decree will be established. If it God's will for sicknesses to consume our health, He wouldn't have anointed Christ Jesus to heal the sick and deliver them from the bondage of infirmity. Don't be afraid of refusing to be ill and claiming perfect health as God is healthy. Dream big, aim big, believe big and finally achieve big stuff.

Acts 10:38 How God anointed Jesus of Nazareth with the Holy Ghost and with power: who went about doing good, and healing all that were oppressed of the devil; for God was with him.

This is one of the most dangerous, false doctrines that one could ever dwell on in his or her daily life, as pertaining to power. The truth is that all power is accessible to all who are in Christ. It is not for any special few or some "great" men. There are obviously those that have been raised by God to lead the rest of us, but this doesn't mean that we need their license or permission to operate in the realm of power. They are to lead, guide and even anoint us for purposes of fulfilling our God-given mandates in life. It is God's wisdom to have order in the body of Christ. They are to and should teach us, guide us and can even be used of God to anoint us and this is wisdom.

God exerted His power within Jesus Christ and further, raised us in Him for His glory on earth. When you use the power of God in Jesus name, it brings Him glory all the more and this is what pleases Him.

Acts 3:16 And his name through faith in his name hath made this man strong, whom ye see and know: yea, the faith which is by him hath given him this perfect soundness in the presence of you all.

This Kingdom, that we belong to now, is a Kingdom of powerful citizens. Its citizens are empowered with the power that makes them able enough to tread underfoot any other false system, thus enforcing the reclaimed dominion. This is also because we are in a spiritual war that will end at the second coming of Christ Jesus. A Christian needs power for all the areas of his or her life. As an example for one to successfully raise children, these days, a parent requires the requisite power to protect his or her children from the snares of this world. We have the spirit of power and not one of frailty *2 Timothy 1:7 For God hath not given us the spirit of fear; but of power, and of love, and of a sound mind.*

All the Christians who believe that doing miracles isn't possible today or that that docket is for the elite few or for those who have walked with God a long time, seen angels or such like are simply misguided.

In Christ Jesus there are no weaklings for He is a strengthener. Those who are referred to as weak, are actually just persons that haven't realized, through faith, the potential within them or are yet to mature in the Lord. However, there are persons that have simply rejected the understanding, that being in Christ is the license to use this power in His name. We must also understand that healing the sick and delivering people from demonic oppression aren't the only uses for this power. It is for your daily living and should be included in everything that you do in wisdom.

Acts 3:16-17 And his name through faith in his name hath made this man strong, whom ye see and know: yea, the faith which is by him hath given him this perfect soundness in the presence of you all. And now, brethren, I wot that through ignorance ye did it, as did also your rulers.

c) Power is given

Luke 10:19 Behold, I give unto you power to tread on serpents and scorpions, and over all the power of the enemy: and nothing shall by any means hurt you.

Let me shed light this fact about power; that no one had or has it originally in his or her human status. No one was originally born with power regardless of how great he or she is. Everyone started off as a normal person until the power of God was placed within him or her. This is how a former thug or even witchdoctor, at God's choosing and timing, by no human understanding, is suddenly transformed into a soul-wining force for the Living God. Power is in God's hand and He gives it to the one He chooses to through His own divine design.

> *Daniel 2:20 ...Blessed be the name of God for ever and ever: for wisdom and might are his:...... 23 I thank thee, and praise thee, O thou God of my fathers, who hast given me wisdom and might,*

A classic case example that I will use to show forth this truth, is the case of the first human Adam. After God formed him and breathed life into him; though alive and in the image of his Creator: God had to give him the power to reign in the garden. Nothing was subject to him because of being created in God's image but rather because of power God gave him.

> *Genesis 1:27-28 So God created man in his own image, in the image of God created he him; male and female created he them. And God blessed them, and God said unto them, Be fruitful, and multiply, and replenish the earth, and subdue it: and have dominion over the fish of the sea, and over the fowl of the air, and over every living thing that moveth upon the earth.*

We do clearly see that Adam had to wait for God to empower him, before he started any work. Furthermore, God restricted him to various sectors of the garden.

> *1 Chronicles 29:12 Both riches and honour come of thee, and thou reignest over all; and in thine hand is power and might; and in thine hand it is to make great, and to give strength unto all.*

The supremacy of our God dictates that only He knows everything that is going on. He alone is the author and the finisher of all things. It is He that will decide when everything will come to a close. Permit me to stress on the word ALONE; it practically means that no other can author or finish anything. Everything is contained within Him, in His absolute status.

Many people are torn between our God and the other gods, who also seem to be powerful. This school of thought is a product of possessing little knowledge of our God resulting into little faith and finally, little or hardly any power.

What happens to us who are in Christ, is the receiving of access to the incomparably mighty power of God *Ephesians 1:19 And what is the exceeding greatness of his power to us-ward who believe, according to the working of his mighty power,* enabling us to function uniquely in our everyday life and to also influence others too. Our former nature was a nature of weakness and defeat. Our current nature, as believers, is of God and powerful beyond description. Paul told the Corinthians that the kingdom of God isn't about words but of power, for this is the nature of our God's. All who have become His children do inherit this power that helps us to dominate the earthly power. This is why you can change circumstances through prayer.

1 Corinthians 4:20 For the kingdom of God is not in word, but in power.

Regardless of walking with Jesus, the Apostles didn't have any power until it was given to them by Jesus. How could they have it yet it is the one with power that is the one to give it? It is through having the Holy Spirit, resident within us, that we possess power that we may impart into others or pray to God on their behalf that they may also receive it. It was never ours, originally, as humans.

Mathew 10:1 And when he had called unto him his twelve disciples, he gave them power against unclean spirits, to cast them out, and to heal all manner of sickness and all manner of disease.

d) Power is asked for

Acts 4:29-31 And now, Lord, behold their threatenings: and grant unto thy servants, that with all boldness they may speak thy word, By stretching forth thine hand to heal; and that signs and wonders may be done by the name of thy holy child Jesus. And when they had prayed, the place was shaken where they were assembled together; and they were all filled with the Holy Ghost, and they spake the word of God with boldness.

It is an official subject, in our knowledge, that Jesus Christ declared that He gave us the power to trample over snakes and scorpions. Both symbolisms do represent *demonic forces and systems*. However, it should also be in our understanding, that the things of God are accessed or brought into effect through the mode of asking in prayer. Asking is the process that brings about the supernatural connection to the power source. Through prayer, the Bible ceases to be a collection of tales of miracles and becomes a real, tangible reality to the one that asked through prayer.

Asking is a most important factor in our lives; it virtually encompasses all the relevant and the seemingly irrelevant areas of our lives. It is a simple truth that the one who asks a lot more, in faith, shall actually have a lot more in the visible but to the one who asks less always has less.

The action of asking God for something in prayer is the peak display of your faith. It shows and proves your relationship with God. Why would you ask for something if you didn't believe that the one you are asking of it from can give it to you? Asking, furthermore, displays your depth of understanding of God. When you ask God for power, it means that you have already comprehended that He is who He says He is and that He alone can truly give power.

Some people go for dark arts because according to their understanding, that is the true source of power. Asking from God shows that you understand that all these other sources of power are false. It also indicates that you are entrusting yourself into His custody because you understand, that there isn't any other that can do what you need Him to do. Asking God for power further proves, that you have completely analyzed life and come to the conclusion that only He can enable you.

Power is requested for from God in order for us to function or live according to His word and it strengthens our relationship with Him. Asking, displays knowledge, not ignorance; desire, not neediness. Asking means and confirms that you do understand that there is a need that should be urgently dealt with in the wisdom of God and not man's. It portrays that you know that you will be able, through God's power, to handle that situation. You are basically saying this, *"Father, here I am, I believe that you hear me and if you enable me to move these mountains, I will move them for your glory."* It also shows that you are ready to move into that new level in the spiritual and physical hierarchy.

e) Power has to be received

*Acts 4:31 And when they had prayed, the place was shaken where
they were assembled together; and they were all filled with the
Holy Ghost, and they spake the word of God with boldness ....: 33
And with great power gave the apostles witness of the resurrection
of the Lord Jesus: and great grace was upon them all.*

The principle of receiving is the twin to the principle or asking. This is because you receive even before you ask, by faith of course. Besides knowledge that there is a need and the one who has been asked had the capacity to provide that which was requested of Him, the one who asks believes that he or she has been granted the request. It means that you, the one asking are now ready to live in a different system of life in accordance with the new resources received through asking. If what you need is strategic strength for business success, when it is received, you will start functioning differently from then onwards.

*Mathew 7:7 Ask, and it shall be given you; seek, and ye
shall find; knock, and it shall be opened unto you:*

Besides being the faith twin to asking, receiving is the follow-up stage after implementing the strategy of asking. Receiving means that the power you didn't have has now been given to you or placed within your sphere of control. You can now manage it freely without looking for it or asking for it. It has now become yours and you are accountable for it but not to it. Many people, due to not having the faith to receive, keep pestering God though He had already released it to them. This has resulted in people who have, living as people who don't have.

The receiving of power fills the space that powerlessness had occupied before you asked and received power. It may be a promise from God that we should have power, but we must activate that promise through asking and then receiving. Receiving can be termed to be the same as taking hold of God's answer thereby changing your life entirely. Receiving of power can be likened to the acquisition of a driving license after attending driving school making you a legitimate driver.

f) Taught on how to use

*Titus 1:9 Holding fast the faithful word as he hath been taught, that he may
be able by sound doctrine both to exhort and to convince the gainsayers.*

*Psalms 32:8-9 I will instruct thee and teach thee in the way which
thou shalt go: I will guide thee with mine eye. Be ye not as the horse,
or as the mule, which have no understanding: whose mouth must
be held in with bit and bridle, lest they come near unto thee.*

Teaching, as a process, isn't for fools but only for the wise. Teaching will evidently make the simple mind able and well equipped. The process of teaching may as well be the only true way of sharpening a person's requisite abilities and skills for better performance in any field. Without teaching, whether through experience or mainstream methods, the exercising of the power of God will be in futility. It is only through this process that one becomes a laser-beam exerciser of the power of God; the executing of duties assigned to one, with the Holy Spirit's inspired precision.

Power isn't and shouldn't be vaguely applied for anything. It is for the specifically intended purpose, requiring one to understand the system well. Let me use church as an example; an Apostle's system is different from an usher's or security officer's system; though they all have the same Holy Spirit. The Holy Spirit empowers these individuals differently, due to their unique roles. This also is the reason for and dire need for mentorship. Good knowledge, acquired through proper training, will make one a maestro in the manifestation of power.

*1 Corinthians 9:26 I therefore so run, not as uncertainly;
so fight I, not as one that beateth the air*

Power in the absence of proper teaching is what leads to corruption, which is already quite rife in the various areas of life e.g. political leadership. Untrained, yet powerful, men misuse power by not applying it for the betterment of the body of Christ. Because he or she wasn't adequately taught, the principles of the proper usage of power, he or she ends up lording over the flock or others.

g) Power is for its designated purpose

*Luke 10:19 Behold, I give unto you <u>power to tread on
serpents and scorpions</u>, and over all the power of the
enemy: and nothing shall by any means hurt you.*

*Mark 3:14-15 And he ordained twelve, that they should be
with him, and that he might send them forth to preach, And
to <u>have power to heal sicknesses, and to cast out devils:</u>*

*Mark 6:7 And he called unto him the twelve, and began to send them
forth by two and two; and gave them <u>power over unclean spirits;</u>*

I have met with many people that use power for the wrong purposes, though sometimes, they do seem right. Power, as we shall also see, later in this book, is meant for the specific purpose only. No one, that has power, should use it for any other purpose besides the intended one, hence the need for instructions. Instructions do guide us on how to operate towards the intended target and not away from it. Also bearing in mind, that we are here for a particular purpose which is God's will and failure to do that will, is simply called; falling short of the mark. This is also actual sinning.

Unlike what many people feel or think about the restrictiveness of instructions they are far from that; instead, they are actual aids towards a good end. We receive from our loving Father of heavenly lights blessings through His power, accessed through instructions. Human nature as we know it is generally rebellious; hence, God protects us from it (*flesh*) through instructing us.

*James 1:17 Every good gift and every perfect gift is from
above, and cometh down from the Father of lights, with
whom is no variableness, neither shadow of turning.*

Power is manifested itself in various ways in regard to the area that it is needed and applied. Power needed in politics is different from power needed at the pulpit and power in sports is different from the head teacher's power in schools. We must use power for the right reasons only. As I state these examples, you need to have in mind the fact that power has to be used and not stored up somewhere. Power doesn't gather interest rates in any bank accounts. Power has to constantly bring in returns and it's on these returns that we are and will be judged.

> *Mark 6:12-13 And they went out, and preached that men should repent. And they cast out many devils, and anointed with oil many that were sick, and healed them.*

> *1 Corinthians 3:13 Every man's work shall be made manifest: for the day shall declare it, because it shall be revealed by fire; and the fire shall try every man's work of what sort it is .... :15 If any man's work shall be burned, he shall suffer loss: but he himself shall be saved; yet so as by fire.*

In the verses above, we are given a clear understanding of what transpires between God and us concerning the subject of power. The Apostles had been with Jesus Christ, who had and has all power, but they themselves didn't have it. However, He later bequeathed them this power (*dunamis*) after which, He specifically instructed what it was for and that they were required to use it specifically for that. Anything outside of this instruction would be acting against God's desire.

In another area, we see the usage of power in a demonic system for a particular reason. Remember this, that it is called a demonic power system because of who the user received it from. He used it to bewitch and mesmerize people. This system is used to manipulate people's lives using satanic forces. It is simply called witchcraft. In any case, whether used for good or for bad, power is for the achievement of a particular goal or end result.

> *Acts 8:9 But there was a certain man, called Simon, which beforetime in the same city used sorcery, and bewitched the people of Samaria, giving out that himself was some great one:*

h) Can be acquired through demonic associations

2 Chronicles 33:6 And he caused his children to pass through the fire in the valley of the son of Hinnom: also he observed times, and used enchantments, and used witchcraft, and dealt with a familiar spirit, and with wizards: he wrought much evil in the sight of the LORD, to provoke him to anger.

I can bet that we have all heard of witches, magicians, astrologers and such kinds of people. There are people who claim to believe that there isn't anything like witchcraft and that it's all in the mind. This is incredibly wrong. Witchcraft does indeed exist and the practitioners have the spiritual power to capture people's thoughts and to manipulate, through hexes, the others' lives. These are all products of demonic powers which are acquired through demonic associations.

We did witness magicians opposing Moses, who had the power of God, when working to free the people of Israel. They used their dark arts believing that the gods of Egypt were in control. These gods, we must note, were and are actually demons under guise.

Exodus 7:11 Then Pharaoh also called the wise men and the sorcerers: now the magicians of Egypt, they also did in like manner with their enchantments.

This situation comes into existence when a person decides to seek out the devil, for power, through demonic enablement to do feats that are superhuman. Power is one of the snares the devil uses; whether it's for spiritual or earthly purposes. Witchcraft is growing in strength today because of the children of God are weak in power. God's people haven't developed in the subject of power hence demonic forces are gaining control by the hour. The fact is that God needs to work His power through us, by faith, to shut down demonic activities in people's lives. It is time to pull down the strongholds that the darks arts practitioners have built and cause many to believe in the name of Jesus Christ.

Acts 13:8-11 But Elymas the sorcerer (for so is his name by interpretation) withstood them, seeking to turn away the deputy from the faith. Then Saul, (who also is called Paul,) filled with the Holy Ghost, set his eyes on him, And said, O full of all subtilty and all mischief, thou child of the devil, thou enemy of all righteousness, wilt thou not cease to pervert the right ways of the Lord? And now, behold, the hand of the Lord is upon thee, and thou shalt be blind, not seeing the sun for a season. And immediately there fell on him a mist and a darkness; and he went about seeking some to lead him by the hand.

We do understand through the case of Simon the sorcerer in the book of Acts chapter 8; that the people believed that he had a great power, even deeming it to be of God; which was false. It was demons that enabled him to work those miracles. This stopped when one with the power of God came to Samaria. Demonic tricks will continue duping people until a child of God, possessing his Father's power, steps into the scene and shuts them down for God's glory.

i) Power dwells within the person

Micah 3:8 But truly I am full of power by the spirit of the LORD, and of judgment, and of might, to declare unto Jacob his transgression, and to Israel his sin.

Luke 4:14 And Jesus returned in the power of the Spirit into Galilee: and there went out a fame of him through all the region round about.

Mark 5:28-30 For she said, If I may touch but his clothes, I shall be whole. And straightway the fountain of her blood was dried up; and she felt in her body that she was healed of that plague. And Jesus, immediately knowing in himself that virtue had gone out of him, turned him about in the press, and said, Who touched my clothes?

One of the most sensitive elements of power is its location. Earthly power, which is vested in any position e.g. minister, is exercised by the legal office-holder while in office. When the person's legal term is done and, he or she leaves the office, the power he or she possessed is left behind. However, heavenly power or God's power is vested in the man and not the office. It's the man who will either make the office weak or powerful by what is contained within him. Phillip did major miracles and revivals yet he wasn't an apostle but a deacon. It wasn't about the office, but rather him the believer according to his faith. He ended up being a groundbreaking evangelist too.

This is the reason why there are so many Apostles today, but there is little or no demonstration of power. Furthermore, they don't all have an equal measure of power. Some do greater things for the glory of God whereas some hardly do a supernatural thing to bring God His glory through baring the title. The supernatural is the evidence of God's authority functioning within a mortal. Miracles are there to follow the child of God and not the child of God to follow the miracles. They should occur because of the child of God has caused them to occur.

Mark 16:17 And these signs shall follow them that believe;

j) Power is evident

Luke 10:17 And the seventy returned again with joy, saying,
Lord, even the devils are subject unto us through thy name.

Psalms 78:12-13 Marvellous things did he in the sight of their fathers, in
the land of Egypt, in the field of Zoan. He divided the sea, and caused
them to pass through; and he made the waters to stand as an heap.

The power of God is not a matter that can be concealed in any manner. Power, in its very nature, is loud and self confirming or self approving. We all know that a president does have earthly power, he doesn't have to say it, the presidential title speaks for itself. It doesn't need to be proven by any other means for it produces its own evidence noticed within the results of its usage. When a man becomes the president, he ceases to be normal anymore.

Paul the Apostle declared that he didn't go to the Corinthians or Thessalonians with mere words only but with the demonstration of power. The one who has power doesn't talk about it but demonstrates it. Power has to cease existing as a part of the Bible stories and should start being manifested in your daily life.

1 Thessalonians 1:5 For our gospel came not unto you in word only, but also in power, and in the Holy Ghost,

1 Corinthians 2:4 And my speech and my preaching was not with enticing words of man's wisdom, but in demonstration of the Spirit and of power:

It is a fact that all the powerful confrontations that took place, as noted in the Word of God, were as a result of faith in God and not through any other mysterious methods. Simply put, all that you need today in order to experience the reality this power same as those in the Bible, is to implement your faith in our God, Jehovah El-Shaddai. This isn't a revelation from me but a direct instruction from our Lord Christ Jesus. God will show Himself through you, His child, when you choose to bring Him glory in this world as it is in heaven. Implementing what you have believed. It doesn't end with having faith; that is the first stage. There is the following stage of implementing the believed issue.

Mark 11:21-24 And Peter calling to remembrance saith unto him, Master, behold, the fig tree which thou cursedst is withered away. And Jesus answering saith unto them, Have faith in God. For verily I say unto you, That whosoever shall say unto this mountain, Be thou removed, and be thou cast into the sea; and shall not doubt in his heart, but shall believe that those things which he saith shall come to pass; he shall have whatsoever he saith. Therefore I say unto you, What things soever ye desire, when ye pray, believe that ye receive them, and ye shall have them.

k) Power is only for the bold

Joshua 1:9 Have not I commanded thee? Be strong and of a good courage; be not afraid, neither be thou dismayed: for the LORD thy God is with thee whithersoever thou goest.

I do know that there is a lot of material on the subject of boldness or rather, fear. However, I do strongly feel in my heart that this subject is yet to be exhaustively dealt with. I am observing this from the perspective of growth; the room to nurture and be nurtured well. Allow me to use a long-route to get to my main statement.

I do understand that people have differing temperaments and variant natures. Some are born tall, others short and this is the same with boldness or the absence of fear. Not everyone is born bold and fierce for some are genuinely, natural cowards. They don't have a strong stomach for most of the things that are considered as mainstream evidence of courage. Society overlooks the more important things about boldness; things like, forgiving, giving true love and sharing out of a pure heart. However, when dealing with power, boldness is a standard requirement.

It is the fuel that ensures your power vehicle is moving well all the time. Without boldness, all the power that you have will be rendered static.

However, I do not seek to pronounce any disqualifications to those who aren't so *bold* at the moment. Timidity simply means that one has a chance to become bold through the right mechanics. I simply need us all to be at par in the understanding that; regardless of where you start from or how you are right now, through the Holy Spirit's help you will develop courage. Our God is a strengthener; to those who rely on Him. It is actually He who makes the weak strong and the cowards bold. Just trust in Him and He will strengthen you mightily beyond your very expectations as He has promised in His Word.

Psalms 119:28 My soul melteth for heaviness:
strengthen thou me according unto thy word.

Let's briefly observe from Prophet Moses' life, when God desired to use him, to carry out freedom duties for the children of Israel; God had to first deal with Moses' little inhibitions and fears. He had to renew and reinvigorate Moses so that he could accomplish the mighty task of delivering of the children of Israel. It is exciting to note, that this man Moses was the same one that had killed an Egyptian enslaver forty years earlier. We don't see him repenting concerning it; the guilt was still with him.

I do wonder where he got the courage to kill the Egyptian enslaver in the first place. Maybe it was just a rush of adrenalin, fuelled by the aggression he had witnessed or the Holy Spirit's prompting. Whichever way, Moses had the traits of cowardice within him at the time of being called, requiring God to embolden him first. This is the same with all who desire to move in power; they must first be bold. Fear will kill anything good if allowed to flourish.

My spiritual father, Apostle Francis Musili, is a man in whom God has invested great power and authority. Though we don't often communicate with many words, for we are action oriented; he once gave me a piece of advice that has carried me all this way and through so much. These are *(present continuous tense)* his words to me, "Pastor Erick, in this life you have to be faithful at all cost. You must also be bold and courageous." This is the key to the success I have had in my ministry. I needed to be courageous enough to venture into a new level of the miraculous.

There isn't any great achiever who achieved anything while operating under the yoke of fear. It is through faith in God that a man becomes courageous. You must allow the spirit of boldness to envelope your entire life if you desire to move in power. Fear causes us to discredit the instructions that God gives us. Only through the bold; holder of God's Word can flourish in power.

> *2 Timothy 1:7 For God hath not given us the spirit of fear;*
> *but of power, and of love, and of a sound mind.*

3. WHY INSTRUCTIONS?

Isaiah 28:26 For his God doth instruct him to discretion, and doth teach him.

Now that we've arrived at the area of instructions, I have indeed noticed that most people do respond to instructions as limiting, controlling items. Instructions are falsely believed to confine people's wills to a specific systems, thus many seek to break away by and subsequently defying them. This is why we have many cases of rebelliousness manifesting in various natures or capacities. Teenagers rebel because instructions seem to be oppressive; they believe that they are being deprived of their freedom to make their choices. Most of the older people are far worse for they do various crimes ranging from cheating at work places, to economic corruption amongst many others.

Many workers today, within the workplace, believe in cheating the system especially during employment. Instructions or rules may as well top the hated things list within the society regardless of age-group or culture. Most weren't taught, when growing about the benefits of instructions, but rather, were forced to follow. It isn't rare to hear a parent telling the child that he or she knows what's best for the child instead of explaining the contentious subject in a coherent language. This makes a child feel small and wish to grow up quickly so that he or she will do what he or she want.

Well, instructions within the Kingdom of God are way more than just commands. They are beyond putting people in these "confines" that many have wrongly believed instructions do. Instructions within the kingdom of God do far much more. In fact, it's instructions that get us free, keep us free and establish us in this freedom. Our salvation is a product of obedience to or of an instruction, Jesus Christ followed God's instruction to come and die for us, on the Cross, willingly. Had He been rebellious, we wouldn't have had this good reality called Salvation. Regardless of all His glory, He still followed instructions from our God. it wasn't a command from God but a loving instruction.

John 8:28 ...... and that I do nothing of myself; but as my Father hath taught me, I speak these things. 29 And he that sent me is with me: the Father hath not left me alone; for I do always those things that please him.

Why instructions?

While establishing about instructions, we must commence with the recognition of who we are and who Our God is. Our God is the Creator of the heavens, the earth and everything thereof. His comprehension is beyond angels' and man's; not forgetting the already condemned demons'. There is none that can be at par with Him. God, therefore, in His infinite wisdom, uses instructions for many things, a few of which I will note herein in this chapter and more as we progress in this book. It is through His instructions that He equips man and angels with part of this infinite wisdom. So that we may all have an understanding of Him, pleasing Him in the process. Herein are some reasons as to why instructions are important;

a) To guide

Psalms 43:3 O send out thy light and thy truth: let them lead me; let them bring me unto thy holy hill, and to thy tabernacles.

To guide is to show someone how to get to a particular place, how to achieve something special or determine the direction of travelling.

If something wasn't special, important or was already known to the instructee, then one basically wouldn't need the instructions then.

God's instructions are one of God's ways of pointing His people in the right direction. It is through instructions that God shows or reveals where one is to rightly end up. Contrary to popular negative thinking, instructions from God are actually His way of proving His love for us.

Elijah was told where to go for food in order to be sustained during the three and a half years of famine. Though the end result was food, he got there through being given specific details, through instructions, from the Lord. God instructed him to go to Zarephath. Here is the breakdown of that set of instructions; go to Zarephath, I have prepared a widow to feed you (*the instruction*); the widow and the feeding (*the details*).

> *1 Kings 17:8-10 And the word of the LORD came unto him, saying, Arise, get thee to Zarephath, which belongeth to Zidon, and dwell there: behold, I have commanded a widow woman there to sustain thee. So he arose and went to Zarephath. And when he came to the gate of the city, behold, the widow woman was there....*

Without God's instructions, we will neither get to where He needs us to get to nor achieve what He desires us to achieve. It is through His instructions to us that He expresses His loving interest as the Chief Stakeholder in our daily well being.

> *Exodus 13:21And the LORD went before them by day in a pillar of a cloud, to lead them the way; and by night in a pillar of fire, to give them light; to go by day and night:*

Without instructions, we shall be as blind people, limited in our progress. We shall be constantly beating about the bushes, failing and falling into the snares orchestrated by the devil. God loves us too much to leave us without guidance. He understands our weaknesses and our need for His involvement in our lives as the leading authority. He can only lead instructed people.

b) To avoid wastage

> *John 6:12 When they were filled, he said unto his disciples, Gather up the fragments that remain, that nothing be lost.*

It is only proper and relevant to understand, that everything belongs to Our God; regardless of whether the one to whom it "*belongs*" believes and calls on the name of Jesus Christ or not. Nothing originally belongs to man, for even his own very breath is given to him or her. Therefore, it is prudent to understand the need for instructions in the field of resource usage or maximisation.

Our God has never been one that makes *"useless"* or *"disposable"* resources. Everything created, is for a particular purpose and it should be made proper use of in line with that purpose. There is a reason why Jesus had twelve Apostles initially and later had the one that had fallen away replaced. After the people had eaten the multiplied bread and fish, Jesus Christ further instructed that the remaining pieces be neatly gathered up. This was for the purpose of avoiding wastage. In order to know why it exists and how to utilize a specific resource; one will need His instructions concerning the specific resource. This is about the Creator's purpose for the creation; made known to you the caretaker.

Time, money, physical energy and all the other resources, should be utilized properly for maximum productivity. This indeed is the case even with those within the secular or worldly areas. Imagine a singer, who doesn't follow instructions about voice utilization; he or she will end up straining and being unproductive. The world, over the centuries, has been awash with talented sportsmen who failed to partake of their careers to the fullest, simply because they couldn't hold onto their coaches or managers instructions. They couldn't use their talents (*resources*) to the maximum, for they either weren't well instructed or disregarded instructions.

c) To equip with knowledge

Genesis 2:17 But of the tree of the knowledge of good and evil, thou shalt not eat of it: for in the day that thou eatest thereof thou shalt surely die.

Instructions are a fragment of the mind of the one that gives them. You can only or better understand the mind of the one that gives the instructions only after he or she issues them. It is the issuer who bears the task of creating complete awareness of them (the instructions). You can only work together with your leader, effectively, when you know and follow your leader's instructions. When your leader instructs you to kill;

it shows you the mindset he has concerning the life of what he wants you to kill same as when he instructs you to preserve life.

We can only do what God needs us to do when we know, agree to and understand His given instructions about the duty at hand. The Apostles knew what Jesus Christ wanted after He gave them the relevant instructions concerning what was needed. They knew what the power He gave them was for, only after He gave the instructions about it and not before that. Had He not clearly indicated to them, through instructions, what His belief of human life was, they would have gone out seeking their own glory using His power.

Summarily, God's instructions allow us to discover and have a good understanding of the heart of God, giving us the opportunity to please Him, having a relationship with Him; built through obedience. Instructions aren't limited to duty only; for Jesus Christ didn't come to make workers but a family. They concern our entire existence.

Let me the blind man, in John 9, as the study example. Jesus healed the man but He didn't do it conventionally. Instead, He put mud on the man and told him to go wash a distance away. In His mind, Jesus planned healing for the man. The blind man, on the other hand, didn't even comprehend what was happening to him; it was through following instructions that he came to understand what was on Jesus' mind concerning him.

4. INSTRUCTIONS ARE RECEIVED

Exodus 3:10-11 Come now therefore, and I will send thee unto Pharaoh,
that thou mayest bring forth my people the children of Israel out of Egypt.
And Moses said unto God, Who am I, that I should go unto Pharaoh,
and that I should bring forth the children of Israel out of Egypt?

Before we delve deeper into this chapter, I believe that we should understand the difference between instructions and principles. Your principles are the personal rules that you use to govern your life. They can be developed from pieces of advice or instructions that you received and were beneficial to you. However, these principles cannot simply become instructions to others besides you. When you practice an instruction as a personal governing system, it may eventually develop from the status of instructions and into principles. Instructions guide you to a desired end but principles govern your everyday life.

Furthermore, instructions are for effective task performance but principles are for self-governance. Though instructions do help, it is principles that play the major role in character formation. You can have a person with a weak character giving instructions to one with strong character. Picture this, a corrupt minister subordinated by a God-fearing assistant minister. Principles are emulated but instructions are obeyed.

It is a confirmed fact that we do have a great number of people who have self-given instructions. How many men of God claim to be called, but weren't called at all. They easily state, that God said or they saw in a dream something to do with that the work they are doing which isn't time. The result of this; is half-baked congregations, visionless and powerless ministries or multiple failures, producing severe frustration. They proclaim works that God hasn't confirmed and this is why the Church of Christ Jesus is so weak today. These are self-sent, self-made personalities who our God has never confirmed as His, are trying to drag the Church down but of course, they will fail, for the church is built on the shoulders of Christ Jesus not on man.

> *Jeremiah 23:21 I have not sent these prophets, yet they ran:*
> *I have not spoken to them, yet they prophesied.*

In the matter of instructions, we should learn from the early Church that none of them designated unto him or herself any post that he or she hadn't been called to. Stephen and Phillip remained deacons regardless of the power of God functioning incredibly within their lives. The great miracles that the Spirit wrought through them didn't change their posts. They were called as and instructed to deacon work and the work at hand was always most important. In general Law, we can call this, functioning in ultra-vires (*functioning outside of one's legally allowed scope*). We do see, after the persecution, God working mightily through Phillip in the field of Evangelism due to his initial humility and obedience.

True instructions aren't created within a person. An instruction is a directive from one who is superior, to another who is subordinate. The instruction will enable the subordinate person to carry out a task to the specifications of the superior. What is within the instructed person is the grace to obey the instructor. Where there is no grace to obey, rebelliousness will flourish greatly. Jesus proved this to be true in *John 8:28-29*. Even as The Son, He still received instructions from God. Never did He simply decide to do whatever He wanted though He could have.

> *And he that sent me is with me: the Father hath not left me*
> *alone; for I do always those things that please him.*

This is the very system that should apply in our lives. We shouldn't just generate the instructions that we use to accomplish feats in our daily lives. Please make it a principle to be receptive to and obedient to instructions. This is why God instructs us through His Word (Bible) so that we may mature in our walk with Him. His words (*instructions within scripture*) smoothly become part of our life, finally, forming a core part of our principles. To further elaborate on this, you may have decided that you will always wake up at 5am. When this is done, it becomes your time management principle; a personal, time-governance rule that is now part of your routine. It will eventually influence your perception of others in the area of time.

However, if you always have to wake up at 5am so that you can get to work on time, this will make it obedience to an instruction. You aren't doing it as a principle but rather out of the fear of the repercussions of getting to work late. It is another's orders that are in play.

The instructor gives the recipient power to execute the instructions he or she has issued. A powerless instructor cannot and should not purport to instruct. This is the principle upon which our God has based His instructions issuance. He instructs for He is powerful and promises to enable us, by His Spirit, to execute. Remember the issue of sending out the disciples two by two? Jesus told them that they should take nothing for He would provide through their obedience to His instructions. He had the power, so He did instruct. After we have done what He had instructed; He gets pleased with us and only then, can we ask for anything in His name and He shall do it.

He declared His being pleased with Jesus for Jesus showed obedience and the prioritizing of the work of His Father by agreeing, willingly, to come onto this earth to save us. Those who are in Christ have been given the in-born ability to be receptive to God's instructions. That's why we have a new spirit and a new heart of flesh. The only challenge is that, many don't have sufficient faith to believe that He can and has been speaking to them always.

Ezekiel 36:26, 27 A new heart also will I give you, and a new spirit will I put within you: and I will take away the stony heart out of your flesh, and I will give you an heart of flesh. And I will put my spirit within you, and cause you to walk in my statutes, and ye shall keep my judgments, and do them.

One of the natures of an instruction, from the right source, is it comes with the relevant package of grace and provision for its execution. The task ahead of the instructed person will bow to this grace and power. The grace contained within the instruction subdues the task on behalf of the instructed person. This is the principle that applies even in the worldly system, simpler still, at your very workplace. If you go with your boss' instructions, you win. This is why the one who walks with the king's decree simply needs to tell everyone in his path "the king sent me" and everyone will excuse him or her. Look at these few verses which go in line with having the king's instructions. It's the same subject when God instructs us to do His will, through His Word; His power accompanies us fully.

Ezra 7:21 And I, even I Artaxerxes the king, do make a decree to all the treasurers which are beyond the river, that whatsoever Ezra the priest, the scribe of the law of the God of heaven, shall require of you, it be done speedily,,,,,,,,,,,,,, :26 And whosoever will not do the law of thy God, and the law of the king, let judgment be executed speedily upon him, whether it be unto death, or to banishment, or to confiscation of goods, or to imprisonment.

God's power doesn't react to our instructions, but rather, approves or confirms our actions as per the instructions given. We actually don't instruct God at any time of our lives, even when we ask Him to do something for us and He does it. It is He who gives us His instructions on how to get something from Him, through faith, in the name of Jesus Christ through prayer. He has power packages for all His instructions, for the obedient one to be facilitated by. Instructions naturally, when properly *(according to the requisite capacity)* followed, will give the instructed more favour with the instructor. When the one who gives you instructions has more confidence in you, he or she will place you higher than the disobedient ones.

Mathew 25:21 His lord said unto him, Well done, thou good and faithful servant: thou hast been faithful over a few things, I will make thee ruler over many things: enter thou into the joy of thy lord.

We should further understand that, when the instructor is giving instructions; he or she is simply making use of the investment he or she has invested in the one he or she is instructing. As a youth pastor, I choose who to give an instruction to someone in accordance with the capacity that person has attained under my tutorship. God does the same. He first invests in you, develops your capacity and then, instructs you. He will never instruct you before He puts His Spirit within you. This is all the more the reason why you should never ever doubt your capability at any time, whether in ministry or any other work system. No instructor is foolish enough to give instructions to one that he or she knows can't carryout the instructions duly.

5. THE SHEPHERD AND HIS POWER

John 10:3-4 To him the porter openeth; and the sheep hear his voice: and he calleth his own sheep by name, and leadeth them out. And when he putteth forth his own sheep, he goeth before them, and the sheep follow him: for they know his voice.

John 10:18 No man taketh it from me, but I lay it down of myself. I have power to lay it down, and I have power to take it again. This commandment have I received of my Father.

We have heard much, I believe, concerning Jesus Christ not only being a Shepherd to us but actually, THE SHEPHERD. There are many quotes on how He leads us beside the clear waters, green pastures and that He will never leave us. This is true and also very important to understand. However, in this topic, I won't be dealing with the obvious fact that Jesus Christ is the one who leads us by His Spirit, because I purpose to dwell on the sheep. This is because the sheep are the ones that are in need of the shepherd's guidance.

However, their general wellbeing isn't simply subject to the shepherd's prowess, only, but is also subject to the sheep's ability to follow their shepherd's instructions. Interestingly, you can tell the shepherd's quality from the condition the sheep are in.

Many Christians do look into this subject of being a sheep, from a perspective that is based on the simple knowledge derived from normal animal husbandry. This principle isn't logically wrong; but for a child of God, it is too shaky to build one's life upon since ours is about the knowledge of our God but not basic livestock keeping. It is required of us to grow deeper and deeper in this knowledge as we continue in Salvation or general Christian life.

The Bible as we surely know wasn't written basing on human understanding. Due to this, we certainly shouldn't bank on human understanding to extract the truth therein. It is the futility of using human understanding that causes many Christians to be frustrated. We aren't really human, after all, for we have attained translation into the status of God's children.

John 1:12,13 But as many as received him, to them gave he power to become the sons of God, even to them that believe on his name: Which were born, not of blood, nor of the will of the flesh, nor of the will of man, but of God.

Furthermore, God's understanding of shepherding is heavenly and not of earth. It is guaranteed, that it is the acquired, heavenly understanding alone that will make us effective when employing our God's Word in our lives. The earth, as we see, it together with all its treasures even those yet to be discovered was formed through the heavenly words of a resident of heaven. In short, the earth itself isn't a product of itself but of heavenly knowledge. The sheep's trust in their shepherd can only be established through their deeper knowledge of their shepherd which is built after a good period of being led by that particular shepherd. My trust in God surely wasn't built in a day; it was built over a long period and through numerous challenges through which I proved that I could trust in His saving power.

John 10:14 I am the good shepherd, and know
my sheep, and am known of mine.

It is important that we steadfastly understand the fact that, the Chief shepherd Jesus Christ, is no longer simply ahead of the sheep. He doesn't walk in front of us so that we follow His voice. He isn't walking with us as He did in the flesh with His disciples. This is because He has put His Spirit within us, the sheep and further appointed stewards to edify (to be a house builder, that is, construct or (figuratively) confirm, build, embolden) us. The practical application of frontal leadership isn't sufficient explanation anymore; our Leader leads us through conjoining (come together; take in marriage) us with Himself. He has made us one with the One that gave

Him the sheep and Himself. There is now in place a stronger unifying bond, between the sheep and the Chief Shepherd.

> *John 10:28-30 And I give unto them eternal life; and they shall*
> *never perish, neither shall any man pluck them out of my hand. My*
> *Father, which gave them me, is greater than all; and no man is able*
> *to pluck them out of my Father's hand. I and my Father are one.*

In *John Chapter 14*, Jesus explains to us a very wonderful subject that correlates very well with what He also said in *John Chapter 10*, about His sheep. In *John 14:21*, He instructs that the way to identify His sheep is through their obedience of His commands. This is confirmed by the sheep's practical application of them. This brings to light the aspect of distinction and that God can't be duped on anything concerning His sheep. He can identify them. This is the same issue that took place in Job chapter 1, when the devil went into heaven. God singled Him out from amongst the sons as an intruder for he never did God's will but rather served to derail many from God's will.

However, He does further state that He has poured into His sheep, His Spirit who leads them into all Truth (*fullness of the Godhead; Colossians 2:9*). So herein, we have already established the location from which He leads the sheep, how He leads them and where He desires them to get to. In *Mark 16:19*, we are duly informed that Jesus ascended into heaven which was confirmed when Stephen was about to sleep (*die*). He clearly saw his Lord (Jesus Christ), standing at the right hand of the Father in heaven. This is also in agreement with Colossians 3:2; that Christ is up above with the Father.

> *Colossians 3:1 If ye then be risen with Christ, seek those things*
> *which are above, where Christ sitteth on the right hand of God.*

> *John 14:15 If ye love me, keep my commandments.*

> *Mark 16:19 So then after the Lord had spoken unto them, he was*
> *received up into heaven, and sat on the right hand of God.*

Jesus, our Chief Shepherd, is with our Father in heaven above, yet He also dwells within our hearts through our faith in Him which will be proven only by our carrying out of His Word, under the Holy Spirit's guidance. The principle of obedience to instructions has to be enforced continually. Jesus came through the door of obedience and we cannot be with Him without going through this door. In simplicity, obedience opened our eyes so that we were able to locate this door and it is only through obedience that we shall dwell within.

*Ephesians 3:17 That Christ may dwell in your hearts by
faith; that ye, being rooted and grounded in love,*

This topic however, hasn't been set aside particularly for the purpose of expounding on Christ's current position only, so let us zero in on its agenda; the Shepherd and His power. Don't forget that we have already established that power is the actual ability that one possesses. The level of power that one possesses will determine what that person will accomplish and how effectively he or she will perform it. All power, we must remember, is of God though it is channeled through various entities e.g. angels, demons, men etc. The listing of demons herein may sound a bit blasphemous, but this is simple truth.

Demons are simply fallen angels and possess the same power they were endowed with when created. If they didn't have power we wouldn't have been witnessing all the rot that we see within the society today. When Jesus Christ decreed that all power had been given to Him and further stated that He has given us a kingdom just as He had received one; He simply meant that He has given us power to rule over power. This is why *Ephesians 1:21-22* states to us that He is placed above all rulers, powers and principalities *Far above all principality, and power, and might, and dominion, and every name that is named, not only in this world, but also in that which is to come: And hath put all things under his feet, and gave him to be the head over all things to the church.* These entities are the other power channels. Through obedience to our God, with the Holy Spirit's allegiance, we can also operate above all channels of power too.

> *Luke 12:32 Fear not, little flock; for it is your Father's*
> *good pleasure to give you the kingdom.*

He, Jesus Christ, further stated that He has given us the power to trample over snakes and scorpions. He meant this *"I do know there are many sources of power in which people have put their faith; but I am giving you power that rules over powers"*. He, our Chief Shepherd, decreed that we received this power when the Spirit of God came upon us. This is the power that overrules any and all other sources or kinds of power channels and is only available to those who are already in Christ. This power hasn't been given to us without the relevant instructions on how to operate it. These instructions reveal to us God's intended purpose for this power. The bottom-line is that, all power is received from God; regardless of who is wielding it.

> *Psalms 62:11 God hath spoken once; twice have I*
> *heard this; that power belongeth unto God.*

> *1 Chronicles 29:12 Both riches and honour come of thee, and thou*
> *reignest over all; and in thine hand is power and might; and in*
> *thine hand it is to make great, and to give strength unto all.*

Let me establish two principle points herein about shepherding; there are two kinds of shepherds. The first, is the King or Chief Shepherd and the second is the king's shepherd. Jesus Christ, in this subject, is the King Shepherd whereas the king's shepherd, is the minister or pastor chosen to care for the flock of God on earth. More importantly, both shepherds it must be duly noted, have been given the sheep by God the Father. It is in *John 21:17*, that Jesus instructed Peter to feed His flock for Him. In simple terms, He was saying "Peter, I trust that you will do for my flock what I desire done for them".

This wasn't a mistake, basing on His prayer in *John 17:20-21*. He knows that, as the Chief Shepherd, He would need point men on earth to do the shepherding of His flock on His behalf while He ruled from heaven. Jesus Christ wasn't simply handing over the sheep to someone

He had trained for a period of time for if this was case, then even Judas would have been amongst them. Rather, He was notifying Peter and the rest of us that God trusts us, the brothers of Christ, to do as our firstborn brother did with us, the sheep. Jesus did send Mary to His brethren *John 20:17 Jesus saith unto her, ... but go to my brethren.*

John 21:17 He saith unto him the third time, Simon, son of Jonas, lovest thou me? Peter was grieved because he said unto him the third time, Lovest thou me? And he said unto him, Lord, thou knowest all things; thou knowest that I love thee. Jesus saith unto him, Feed my sheep.

John 17:20-21 Neither pray I for these alone, but for them also which shall believe on me through their word; That they all may be one; as thou, Father, art in me, and I in thee, that they also may be one in us: that the world may believe that thou hast sent me.

When I talk of the shepherd's power, one must make a clear distinction between these two kinds of shepherds. This is because one gives the other power making the receiver subject to the giver. The King Shepherd is far lifted above all thrones, powers, dominions, titles or anything and everything else known and unknown to man, demons and angels alike. He is the one who gives power through His Spirit to His shepherds placing and keeping them far above the thrones, dominions, powers and principalities i.e. believers, the mainstream five-folders and all other stewards of His flock. Without this ability and positioning, the sheep will be vulnerable under their entrusted shepherd's custody.

1 Peter 5:2-3, 4 Feed the flock of God which is among you, taking the oversight thereof, not by constraint, but willingly; not for filthy lucre, but of a ready mind; Neither as being lords over God's heritage, but being ensamples to the flock. And when the chief Shepherd shall appear, ye shall receive a crown of glory that fadeth not away

The delegated shepherds must understand that they need power. This is essentially for the purposes of effective leading the flock of Jesus Christ in their designated areas on earth as we all await Christ's second coming. I feel that I should further explain the issue on Christ's position. Position, is an incredibly sensitive subject because it matters much and ignorance in this subject will mean real failure. (Much as He is in heaven, we are one with Him in Spirit though away from Him, only in the flesh *Ephesians 2:6* and much as He is in heaven, we are still with Him. Though we are apart in the flesh, we are still one with Him *2 Corinthians 5:6-7*).

Ephesians 2:6 And hath raised us up together, and <u>made us sit together in heavenly places in Christ Jesus</u>:

2 Corinthians 5:6 Therefore we are always confident, knowing that, whilst we are at home in the body, we are absent from the Lord: (For we walk by faith, not by sight :)

Now, what does the shepherd and his power mean? It means; the ability that the shepherd has; to guide, feed, protect, nurture and preside over the flock. Jesus Christ, our Chief Shepherd raised the dead, healed the sick and delivered them that were in bondage. He had received the necessary power to do so. I don't remember the Apostles being sickly or downtrodden when walking with Christ. He even said at one time that they didn't need to fast at that time.

He ensured that they were well protected against the devil such that even as He was about to die, He still protected them through prayer in *John Chapter 17*. It is wrong for the sheep to be oppressed by demonic forces yet they have a shepherd watching over them. Being sickly and defeated, for the flock, simply proves that the shepherd is weakly.

A shepherd must have the necessary power to protect the sheep in his or her custody. There is the being in possession of the sheep but not having the ownership of the sheep. I, as a shepherd, am in possession of the sheep that Jesus has given me to nurture but I have never owned them. They aren't my property. I always remember that I am answerable to another for them. The shepherds only work on those who fall within their jurisdiction not those beyond it. The shepherd is there for the benefit of those he or she is ordained to care for.

The term sheep doesn't simply denote or stand for people; instead, it encompasses everything that has been placed within the shepherd's custody. This ranges from the shepherd himself or herself, the shepherd's nuclear family, his talents and gifts etc. It also includes all the kingdom resources given to you by God. My duty as a shepherd isn't simply to ensure that the attackers *(mostly demons)* are kept at bay, but that all kingdom resources are well utilized for the benefit of the sheep also.

> *1 Peter 5:4 And when the chief Shepherd shall appear, ye*
> *shall receive a crown of glory that fadeth not away.*

Wherein, do instructions come in this area of the Shepherd and His power? In order to elaborately answer this question, we have to take the perspective of how the Shepherd relates to His sheep. How He gets to deliver them from wickedness and into the relevant areas which God has preplanned for them to be at. Jesus said in John Chapter 10:4, that His sheep, know His voice and they follow Him; in John Chapter 14:21, He said that those who hear His commands and follow them or do them are His.

Through these key verses, amongst many, we realize that only the sheep that obey the instructions reap the full reward. We only get to be called Christians when it has been proven that we do abide by and live by the instructions of Jesus Christ.

> *John 10:4 And when he putteth forth his own sheep, he goeth before*
> *them, and the sheep follow him: for they know his voice.*

> *John 14:21 He that hath my commandments, and keepeth them,*
> *he it is that loveth me: and he that loveth me shall be loved of my*
> *Father, and I will love him, and will manifest myself to him.*

Now turning onto the shepherd, we should all realize that each shepherd has a specific sphere of influence. It is only Christ Jesus who can influence everything as per His will. This is in regard to Him telling us that through faith all things are possible. What He meant was that it will be only if we apply our faith to achieve that which does please God *(all according to God's desire or that which pleases God, that includes your success).* Furthermore, though studying of the Word, we learn that though God's presence is everywhere, He isn't in everything. This is reflected or proven by the fact that there are those who love Him and those who don't have even the least respect for Him.

It is His instructions that keep us steadfast, in the palm of His hand, such that we get to be sustained beyond the satan's reach. It is only the sheep that stray that become easy prey for the wolves. In *John 10*, Jesus doesn't say that He goes out to look for the wolf, but it is the wolf that comes to attack the sheep in His care. He further explains that He builds a hedge around the sheep, but the robber tries to sneak in. The fact that He can leave the ninety nine to fetch one simply shows us the kind of attention and love that He has; not that we should run outside *Rev 21:15.*

Though He has never been fatigued concerning us, we shouldn't be constantly rebellious, for rebelliousness is same as witchcraft. Our obedience to the instructions of God gets God's power functioning for us, in the name of Jesus Christ. With finality, it is the only obedient sheep which will get to the cool waters and green pastures.

Jesus gave authority to Peter and the others in order for them to overcome the devil and set captives free. The question that we should ask ourselves is this; *"how could mere men achieve so much based on simple words?"* It was due to obedience to these simple words *(instructions),* that they shepherded the early church with power and much tenacity. The early church is recorded to have given itself over *(wholesomely)* to the teachings of the Apostles and to prayer. They prayed to God but also received instructions from the Apostles and this kept them strong.

Today's society is a rebellious one, full of rowdy sheep that never listen such that they have no option of obedience. After obeying the initial call to Salvation, they turn away from the system of obedience and into disobedience. These are sheep with goat mentality. I do agree that, it is also quite hard to find a good caretaker or custodian *(shepherd)* today too.

I challenge you to carryout an observation at the work places today; you won't fail to conspicuously notice that the juniors want to usurp the authority of their seniors even before their time. Many people, who branch out to start their own businesses or ministries do so, not because it is right but simply because they just hunger to be their own bosses. This is the epitome of wickedness, we all have to answer to someone just as another has to answer to us. When we have a society in which none want to answer to another or be accountable to another, we shall end up having anarchy in our hands.

Before we embark on anything special, we must look at Biblical examples for enlightenment. Peter received caretaking authority after he himself and the others had been well nourished. They weren't in a rush to go start ministries after healing or casting out a few demons. They completed their training first so that they could train others. Jesus was a good Shepherd to them. This further proves that if you are a good superior, your subordinates will gladly stick with you until the right time to depart.

Every shepherd has his jurisdiction and it is therein, that he or she has power. We are the flock and should follow our shepherd's instructions lest the wolves devour us. We become sheep in God's pasture because of instructions and nothing else. It is also up to the shepherds to strengthen themselves for the purposes of being depended upon and protecting the sheep at all times.

> *1 Peter 5:2 Feed the flock of God which is among you,*
> *taking the oversight thereof, not by constraint, but*
> *willingly; not for filthy lucre, but of a ready mind;*

6. HIS ROD AND STAFF

Psalms 23:4 ..... for thou art with me; thy rod and thy staff they comfort me.

It is quite amusing, yet true, that Christians mostly remember this part of scripture when either in trouble or when needy of encouragement. For most, this verse's recital is just as far as the going goes. It isn't rare to come across many Christians who say they are waiting on the Lord but in reality, they are simply dejected and have fainted in spirit. They just don't want to sound faithless. However, it will be prudent for us to delve a little deeper, with the Holy Spirit's guidance, of course.

Since we aren't talking about earthly items but heavenly ones; we must first grasp this fact that both the staff and rod indeed do exist. These are actual, practical tools that exist within the Word of God itself. It is common for many to believe theoretically concluding that since the Bible uses a lot of analogies, God didn't really mean an actual rod and a staff. Many tend to overly spiritualise everything according to what they are feeling at a time or simply, want to believe. It is very wise to have a good comprehension of all the analogies or similes that the Lord uses in His Word. This is because His power does reside and move within these, purposefully, for the Christian's manifestation of power.

This can only be understood through the meditation in His Word, diligently. The recipient of instructions must initially understand this fact and its discovery will herald his or her victorious living. Outside of the operation of the Word of God exists nothing but failure and subsequently, God's wrath. The rod and staff are therefore only for those within God's family.

Let us commence with discussing the rod. We are going to discuss the purposes of the rod in a deeper way besides the use of a rod as evidenced in *proverbs 13:24 He that spareth his rod hateth his son: but he that loveth him chasteneth him betimes.* I picked this verse due to its popularity; however, a rod has diverse usages in the Bible. From meaning strength in kingship and family patriarchy the meanings are endless. Besides all these essential usages or meanings, let us concentrate on *Psalms 23* for it is one that makes a direct inference on our Lord who is also our Shepherd. The rod of Christ Jesus is used to rebuke us.

Rebuking in this aspect doesn't mean shutting us down as He used to do with the Pharisees. Rather, it rather means *correction, refutation, proof convict, convince, tell a fault.* This is about progressively and understandingly setting one back onto the right path; this is the path of obedience. The right path is the particular path that leads to the specific area that God wants us to dwell within. We must remember that every instruction that we obey, leads us into a certain area chosen by God. Every instruction has a specific, expected result; moving out of this specific path does warrant the usage of the rod.

Let's use the parable of the talents as an example to further elaborate the contents of the previous paragraph. If the one who doubled his five talents had got four instead of five more; he would have been deemed to have fallen short of the mark thereby sinning. This is because the Word tells us that they were all given the talents according to their capacities. None was given beyond what he could manage. Anytime you perform something below your capacity, you are deemed to have fallen short of the set mark. It is within such circumstances that the Shepherd employs His rod. This action is the action of disciplining us or in a different language, getting us functioning at our full capacity thus bringing God glory.

The rod of the Lord doesn't work like the earthly rods which use the element of the fear of pain in order to enforce discipline. It is a building tool through which we experience the abundance of the love of Christ in correction *(putting things rightly in order)*; if we are obedient enough. His rod isn't used to force us to change but rather, is used to mould use as a porter moulds the clay in what is pleasing. Love and patience, are key in this process. Every caretaker shepherd must learn to use these tools when handling the Lord's sheep.

The staff of the Lord, on the other hand, is the tool that our loving Lord uses, as written, to comfort us. To give us the much needed healing and nourishment in the times of pain or frustrations derived from living in this world. *2 Corinthians 1:3-4 Blessed be God, even the Father of our Lord Jesus Christ, the Father of mercies, and the God of all comfort; Who comforteth us in all our tribulation, that we may be able to comfort them which are in any trouble, by the comfort wherewith we ourselves are comforted of God.* Just as it's not always, that people around us will be pleased with our diligence, so will instructions they don't always please us or appear enjoyable to us.

His staff is used to encourage and revitalize us, so that we shall not give up in our walk to victory. We do know that the challenges we face are there to build us up, but we need to be encouraged on also for sometimes, this isn't clear to us. Encouragement is what shall empower us so that we can joyfully undertake the performance of an instruction which may not be sweet to us. Do you recall the days when God seems too far away, deaf to your cries or ignorant of your pain? Paul gave a statement that encouraged me a lot in the book of 2nd *Corinthians* Chapter 7.

2 Corinthians 7:4-7 Great is my boldness of speech toward you, great is my glorying of you: I am filled with comfort, I am exceeding joyful in all our tribulation. For, when we were come into Macedonia, our flesh had no rest, but we were troubled on every side; without were fightings, within were fears. Nevertheless God, that comforteth those that are cast down, comforted us by the coming of Titus; And not by his coming only, but by the consolation wherewith he was comforted in you, when he told us your earnest desire, your mourning, your fervent mind toward me; so that I rejoiced the more.

The unique issue is that Titus was actually the staff that God used in Paul's situation to strengthen him. The reason why I said earlier on in this chapter that these two items are heavenly or spiritual; is because God can use anything or anyone as a rod or staff just as He used Titus in the above part in Paul's life. We should come to and settle upon the understanding that the Holy Spirit is limited in His operate and so are our spirits when led of the Holy Spirit. You and I can also be encouragement tools unto others by the grace of God.

In the functioning of the rod and staff; it is indeed the Holy Spirit who is in charge or control of our lives. He is the one who has been with custody over our lives by our Lord and Savior Christ Jesus. Furthermore,

He is the one who also enables and will enable us to do God's work or carry out the instructions that we have received. This is proven so through a sequence of events that took in scripture. Let us follow them up so that we can get a clearer understanding. Jesus commissioned them, the Apostles, with a simple looking instruction.

> *Mathew 28:19 Go ye therefore, and teach all nations, baptizing them*
> *in the name of the Father, and of the Son, and of the Holy Ghost:*
> *lo, I am with you alway, even unto the end of the world. Amen.*

He gave them a simple instruction concerning what they would do with their lives and acquired knowledge, after He had ascended into Heaven. We should also remember that He had already highlighted to them the persecutions that they would suffer in His name and for His name. God also confirmed this when telling Ananias about Paul's future suffering for His Word. Jesus knowing this gave them another directive...

> *Acts 1:4 And, being assembled together with them, commanded*
> *them that they should not depart from Jerusalem, but wait for the*
> *promise of the Father, which, saith he, ye have heard of me.*

Finally, to confirm the comfort part, Jesus told us that...

> *John 14:15-18 If ye love me, keep my commandments. And I will pray the*
> *Father, and he shall give you another Comforter, that he may abide with you*
> *for ever; Even the Spirit of truth; whom the world cannot receive, because it*
> *seeth him not, neither knoweth him: but ye know him; for he dwelleth with*
> *you, and shall be in you. I will not leave you <u>comfortless</u>: I will come to you.*

It is therefore now clear that all of us, who follow the instructions of God, do need His rod and staff fully functioning in our lives. The Holy Spirit is the one who uses the rod and staff of God as mentioned in *Psalms 23:4.....*

> *Yea, though I walk through the valley of the shadow of death, I will fear*
> *no evil: for thou art with me; thy rod and thy staff they <u>comfort me</u>.*

7.   FOR OUR OWN OUR PROFITING

*Isaiah 48:17 Thus saith the LORD, thy Redeemer, the Holy
One of Israel; I am the LORD thy God which teacheth thee to
profit, which leadeth thee by the way that thou shouldest go.*

Commonly, we have been taught to describe profiting according
to financial terms or understanding. Money, in many areas of life, has
pitifully become the foundational principle when talking of profiting.
For many it just about what you have gained after transacting; whether
it's a spiritual transaction or physical. How much do I get after sowing
seed? Will I get more after giving to God?

The world of today has become extremely money-minded, resulting
in the choking or absence of God's wisdom in the lives of many.
Marriages today and other family ties are built on money, employees are
majorly motivated by monetary packages; the list of examples is endless.
Philanthropic activities or charitable works, which were once noble,
haven't escaped this money issue. They are mainly done to convince
sponsors to give more money to the *"volunteers."*

However, we need to look into this issue, based on spiritual
enlightenment, which I may refer to as "God-kind" of perspective. It is
only through God's eyes that we perceive reality. Let us therefore go beyond
the normal human concepts, taught basing on limited understanding;
searching out God's reality with the Spirit's help. Profiting is the actual
realization of all of God's goodness in one's life. We must note that most of
the hardships that many face, are results of accepting falsehoods presented
to them as truths. One may have been presented with a false reality that
a situation is too great for him or her so the person decided to commit
suicide in the belief that there wasn't any other way out. Such a great loss,
yet what may have been needed, may have been a little encouragement.

Gaining in life should be a product of God's presence and empowerment. This is the gaining done, not by sweating hard, but rather by the grace of God. This is when God graciously carries you through life in His strength and divine favour. Favour acquired through obedience.

Psalms 127:1-2 A Song of degrees for Solomon. Except the LORD build the house, they labour in vain that build it: except the LORD keep the city, the watchman waketh but in vain. It is vain for you to rise up early, to sit up late, to eat the bread of sorrows: for so he giveth his beloved sleep.

The issue of profiting, in God's eyes, involves His children experiencing the fullness of what He has translated them into. We have to understand how to take a hold of and enjoy this new status in its fullness. We must recall that there was a time that we were not His children or even in good terms with Him. We are products of the wonderful, reconciliatory duty that Jesus Christ successfully carried out on the Cross. Had He quit on the way to Calvary, we wouldn't be calling onto God as we do today and certainly, He wouldn't be fond of us.

This should encourage us to make sure that all the benefits contained in His promises and redemption are partaken of by us. We should further understand that God does love us in a more than literal manner. His love isn't abstract or according to your imagination; it is real. *1Thesalonians 1:4 Knowing (to understand, be aware), brethren beloved, your election of God.*

In relevance to the above quoted verses (*Psalms 127:1-2*), God brings to our understanding that He is the one who enables us to profit (acquire benefits). He teaches us how to gain all the riches and good things available to us; through faith in Jesus Christ. In other words, He is saying that He wants us to understand the full dimension of whom we are and where we are. Throughout my life, I have noticed that there is a seemingly tangible yet invisible wedge between the biblical status of God and His status in the day to day of lives of Christians.

I know this doesn't really sound doctrinal but please indulge me some more and you will understand why I say so. We need to see and experience our God as it is written about Him in His Word. Many have Him verbally, yet fewer, practically. In Hebrews 2; we learn that

God was fully and powerfully active in the lives of the Apostles the same way He was with the prophets of old. The Apostles experienced the remarkable power (*dunamis*) of God in their lives just as they had read about Him. Do you experience the same today or are you asking questions like Gideon?

Hebrew 2:4 God also bearing them witness, both with signs and wonders, and with divers miracles, and gifts of the Holy Ghost, according to his own will?

The scripture is not written for God as many Christians do think but for us; we are the one's that are in need of it. This is God's reason for instructing the children of Israel to write down what He had done for them for it wasn't their children who saw those mighty deeds of God. They wrote them down so that their children, who didn't see, may know and believe in Him. The mighty deeds of God have been written so we may know and experience them too. There are many who believe that quoting scriptures a lot will get God more involved in their lives and do His mighty deeds.

This isn't truth. Scripture is written for us, so that we can have the solid basis for a relationship with our God. It's for action but not theory. It is for us that our loving God has put forth His Word so that we can have a launching pad from which to take off into a new life. It is after we implement His Word (Scripture) that God acts on our behalf. Do not be like Gideon who said that what he had read and heard wasn't what he was experiencing. May you experience God as you have read and heard about Him.

Judges 6:13 ....and <u>where be all his miracles which our fathers told us of, saying, Did not the LORD bring us up from Egypt?</u> but now the LORD hath forsaken us, and delivered us into the hands of the Midianites.

Let's now swim a little deeper. Many Christians still do pray to Jesus Christ with the understanding of His state as a man walking the earth moving from Galilee to Nazareth and all the other towns which He visited. It sounds or feels good and they believe that they are connecting with Him more but this is based on shallow knowledge.

Jesus Christ, whom we worship today, isn't in that old state of walking towards Golgotha, or in need of food and encouragement from our Heavenly Father.

We are now worshipping Him, the risen Jesus Christ, who is highly exalted far above all. He is no longer in the flesh or heading onto Calvary for crucifixion; but is ruling over the whole house of God. He isn't passing by or visiting houses to eat with people or playing the unseen visitor's role today. He is the King of kings who is always with His people, dwelling within them and will never leave them even for a split second. Therefore, have we been doing the wrong thing? Let me answer that in the next paragraph.

Jesus Christ was glorified, has and will always be glorified. He has always been the Son of God and I don't know of any other position that is more glorious than this. His loving action of dying for us didn't change Him, it changed us; *John 17:5 And now, O Father, glorify thou me with thine own self with the glory which I had with thee before the world was.* The power He received, He received on our behalf that in His name we can channel the power of God, even when in our mortal state, receiving heavenly results. His time on earth was simply a phase He went through in God's strategy to get Himself a new family i.e. you and me. Jesus never gave His Life for Himself but gave it up for us; *John 17:3 And this is life eternal, that they might know thee the only true God, and Jesus Christ, whom thou hast sent.*

In John 10:17, Jesus Christ clearly explains that the Father loves Him because He willingly gave His Life though He had the power to pick it up again. This isn't the confession of a broken, needy person, but is the Word of the Mighty One who understood His purpose. In John 1:1-2, the Bible clearly states that the Word was with God and was God *...In the beginning was the Word, and the Word was with God, and the Word was God. The same was in the beginning with God.* He and God were and are inseparable just as we are with Him now. We should never think that Christ lost in order to gain; it's we who had lost, but He came to give it back to us. We shouldn't feel pity for Him when meditating on what He went through; rather, we should rejoice continually that He suffered violently beyond comprehension for our sakes, that we may have what He already had, easily.

God wants us to be able to realize the whole Truth that we have been brought into. Everything pertaining to the Kingdom of light of the Son He loves. We shouldn't miss out on anything good. He also wants us remain above the devil always as Christ already set us according to Ephesians 2:6. *And hath raised us up together, and made us sit together in heavenly places in Christ Jesus.* Now you have your answer to the earlier asked question and Glory to God for His goodness.

In order for us to experience this Truth (reality), God got us His guiding instructions which He concealed in the Bible. This is our compass or navigation device through which we can explore all the corners of this Kingdom. This is what He was telling us through Jeremiah's life in the book of *Jeremiah 33:1-2*; when He informed Jeremiah that He would reveal great and mighty deeds when requested. God later realized that there was still a language and distance barrier so He released Jesus to come to us and get us into the family.

A family has one language and our language is the Word of God as revealed to us by the Holy Spirit. Jesus said that He would lead us into all truth just as He *(the Spirit)* had led Him here on earth. Jesus Christ walked in profit all the days of His life on earth. He walked in this manner through obedience and faith in our God. The same God Jesus prayed to is the same one we pray to today and so, we should experience the same kind of Life through our very own obedience to the instructions of God. Unity with God through His Word can only be enacted by the Holy Spirit.

Ephesians 4:4,5,6 There is one body, and one Spirit, even as ye are called in one hope of your calling; One Lord, one faith, one baptism, One God and Father of all, who is above all, and through all, and in you all.

In Heaven, Jesus Christ doesn't need the Holy Spirit's guidance but that totally different for us on earth. We are clearly instructed that the Holy Spirit, is not only a Teacher but is also the deposit guaranteeing our inheritance. That through the Holy Spirit everything about our new lives will be achieved. All this, surprisingly, is contained in and accessed through instructions. Obeying God's instructions guarantees us our profiting. It is God who teaches us to profit through His instructions contained in His Word by His Spirit. However, we should also comprehend that not everything in the Bible is an instruction, but God's Spirit shows us where His instructions are in Word.

Isaiah 30:21 And thine ears shall hear a word behind thee, saying, This is the way, walk ye in it, when ye turn to the right hand, and when ye turn to the left.

Isaiah 48:17 Thus saith the LORD, thy Redeemer, the Holy One of Israel; I am the LORD thy God which teacheth thee to profit, which leadeth thee by the way that thou shouldest go.

8. FOR GOD'S CONFIRMATION

1 Kings 18:36-39 And it came to pass at the time of the offering of the
evening sacrifice, that Elijah the prophet came near, and said, LORD God
of Abraham, Isaac, and of Israel, let it be known this day that thou art God
in Israel, and that I am thy servant, and that I have done all these things
at thy word. Hear me, O LORD, hear me, that this people may know
that thou art the LORD God, and that thou hast turned their heart back
again. Then the fire of the LORD fell, and consumed the burnt sacrifice,
and the wood, and the stones, and the dust, and licked up the water that
was in the trench. And when all the people saw it, they fell on their faces:
and they said, The LORD, he is the God; the LORD, he is the God.

It becomes pretty clear to one, after intently studying the Word of
God, with the Spirit; that God has never confirmed things which weren't
within His Divine plan or purpose. This is obviously regardless of the
fact that some may seem to bring Him praise. It is wise to understand
that everything He involves Himself in is certainly for His glory. We
do note a lot from the book of Jeremiah, of how, many false prophets
spoke things which sounded glorious about God or prophesied of His
deliverance. He however denied them. Their sweet words from their
deceitful tongues couldn't force Him to approve that which wasn't from
Him. Saying nice things about God, which He didn't send you to speak,
will simply make you His enemy. He will never affirm any falsified
reports even if they were in praise of Him.

Jeremiah 23:25 -26 I have heard what the prophets said, that
prophesy lies in my name, saying, I have dreamed, I have dreamed.
How long shall this be in the heart of the prophets that prophesy
lies? yea, they are prophets of the deceit of their own heart;

God, we must comprehend, has always been in the business of personally commissioning people to carry out particular tasks for Him. There is a data base in heaven which contains all the names of those sent by Him and how they are performing their duties. In sending them out, we do realise that God always attached a promise to the instructions He gave them. He always promised that He would confirm these messengers as executors of His duties. That He would prove that He was the one in charge of whatever that person was doing and that the results were for His glory.

This is one of the reasons why He instructs us to "*test those spirits.*" This strategy will help us understand the kind of spirit that's behind the person's actions. The Spirit behind Elijah's actions was the Holy Ghost of God, therefore, he was found acceptable before God. God, technically didn't have any other choice but to prove Himself true to Elijah. When God personally commissions you, He will be obligated to prove you true by Himself before all.

I discovered something, after looking into some of the greatest miracles in the Scripture, which of course is the basis of our lives. I discovered that each miracle was preceded by an instruction and was further implemented through obedience to that instruction. Our dear Lord and Saviour, Jesus Christ, actually did everything that He did, through instructions. In everything He did you will note that either He fulfilled Scripture by performing something that was written in the Bible or stated that it was the Father's will. Prophet Moses waited for instructions, Gideon, Daniel, Apostle Paul, Prophet Elijah (*the list is long*) also did everything they did after receiving instructions.

Jesus Christ instructed His Apostles on what to do for God in their lives and also made another promise besides the one about Him being with them always. He promised to confirm His Word (*instructions*) that they duly obeyed or performed. Jesus Christ wasn't debating about confirming His Word; but was putting His integrity on the line, that, if they did what He wanted them to do according to His given instructions, He would certainly confirm that they were sent of Him. This wasn't about whether His Word was true or not.

Mark 16:19-20 So then after the Lord had spoken unto them, he was received up into heaven, and sat on the right hand of God. And

they went forth, and preached every where, the Lord working with
them, and confirming the word with signs following. Amen.

It is through the wonderful confrontation, between Prophet Elijah
and the priests of baal, that we do realize that Elijah, though full of faith,
didn't ask God to simply confirm his (*Elijah's*) action's but rather to
confirm that he was carrying out God's plan. That He, God, had chosen
him for that purpose and Prophet Elijah hadn't appointed himself. He
was chosen by God to carry out that duty within the specific instructions
relevant to it. God duty was to confirm that He indeed had sent him.
Moses is another example of one that God answered a prayer for
confirmation from; just as He did for Jesus Christ. Moses stated that
if Jannes and Jambres died a normal death, then God hadn't called him. God
answered him simply for the purposes of showing all, that Moses was
His choice by doing the totally new thing. All these men, asked God to
confirm that the businesses that they undertook, were simply procedural
obedience to God Himself.

Instructions, therefore, are the guidelines that God gives so that He
can use us to prove Himself true to us and to others through our lives.
God won't just confirm any human issue, thought or a product of human
understanding. If you need God to prove Himself true, in your life, His
instructions must come first. This is the reason why we have the mind
of Christ today, in the first place. It must form your foundation. One
may argue that God confirms the words of His prophet as it is written
in *Isaiah 44:26 That confirmeth the word of his servant, and performeth the
counsel of his messengers; that saith to Jerusalem.*

Yes, very true indeed, however, how will one attain servant-hood
status, if not through instructions from Him? It is a fact, that a servant
is only as valuable as his or her capacity to effectively execute received
instructions. You may be weak, sickly or not very talented yet obedience
will keep you afloat. The servant of God will only be approved of God
as per the level or extent of his or her obedience to the Word of God. If
you do wish to see more of God's sovereign power in your life and acquire
your blessings from Him, you must learn to inquire of Him first. This
is wisdom. David excelled through asking for God's opinion first before
charging into battle. His victories were a confirmation of God's promise;

that He will never let those who call on His name to be shamed. It is God who always advised him on what to do or what strategies to implement.

> *2 Samuel 5:23-25 And when David enquired of the LORD, he said, Thou shalt not go up; but fetch a compass behind them, and come upon them over against the mulberry trees. And let it be, when thou hearest the sound of a going in the tops of the mulberry trees, that then thou shalt bestir thyself: for then shall the LORD go out before thee, to smite the host of the Philistines. And David did so, as the LORD had commanded him; and smote the Philistines from Geba until thou come to Gazer.*

God didn't simply answer David with a "yes", He duly instructed him on how to go about the war and achieve victory. *Draw near to me and I will draw nearer to you.* Is another instruction which will help us experience the presence of God. Victory came easily because the instruction was obeyed. God will never allow you to go somewhere without telling you how to get and what to do there. Instructions from God are His assurance of His full commitment and involvement in your affairs. I wish to explain this assuring truth that we don't have to wait to hear the *"still, soft voice,"* in order to know that God has instructed us. Every time you read the Bible, believe in it and apply its information, you officially become obedient and God will confirm Himself in your life through what you have read believingly.

9.   THE BASIS OF OUR RELATIONSHIP

Joshua 22:5 But take diligent heed to do the commandment and the law, which Moses the servant of the LORD charged you, to love the LORD your God, and to walk in all his ways, and to keep his commandments, and to cleave unto him, and to serve him with all your heart and with all your soul.

John 14:15 If ye love me, keep my commandments.

This term, *relationship*, means the existence of *a state of connectedness between people (especially an emotional connection)*. However, what we are seeking through this book is to understand how walking in instructions will cause us to actually walk *(experience)* in God's power. The experiencing of the signs and wonders that we have read about in the Bible, in our lives. This will show us how to get the Mighty Spiritual Word of God to influence or dictate occurrences in our lives by His power.

Every relationship, even the spiritual ones, has a set structure that governs how the parties involved interlink. In this book, I seek to build or bring to light the fact that instructions are the fundamental basis of man's relationship with the Almighty God. How a man on earth, can relate well, with the Lord Almighty who sits on His Heavenly throne of mercy and power. How a weak mortal man, can access the unlimited, mighty power of God resulting to the performance of the impossible with ease. We must always remember this, that all power is in God's hand and He has put in Christ Jesus' custody.

1 Chronicles 29:11 Thine, O LORD, is the greatness, and the power, and the glory, and the victory, and the majesty: for all that is in the heaven and in the earth is thine; thine is the kingdom, O LORD, and thou art exalted as head above all.

Ephesians 1:22- 23 And hath put all things under his feet, and gave him to be the head over all things to the church, Which is his body, the fulness of him that filleth all in all.

We should understand that there are three kinds of relationships which a person may have with God. I am not talking about faith in the context of believing in God for something, but faith that is; Christ Jesus. These are *i)* a weak *ii)* a poor or *iii)* strong relationship. We should also have in mind that faith means persuasion. A weak *(wanting in strength)* relationship is a product of ignorance, deafness to His voice and poor receptiveness to His instructions; maybe due to little knowledge. A poor *(deserving or inciting pity)* relationship, is a product of negativity towards His instructions. You may hear from Him and know what He desires but your attitude is all wrong.

This negativity causes God to be mostly angry and displeased with the person. Lastly, a strong relationship is a product of good listening abilities and total obedience to Him. There is listening, by itself and the listening which includes action, based on what one has heard. One of the results is rejoicing in the Lord always regardless of anything else or prevailing circumstances. *Psalms 37:4 Delight thyself also in the LORD; and he shall give thee the desires of thine heart.*

Philippians 4:4 Rejoice in the Lord alway: and again I say, Rejoice.

Instructions are and will always be the backbone of the kind of relationship that we have with God. The capacity in which we take and apply His instructions will always be the measuring rod. A good relationship with God will always be evident due to the forthcoming fruits of power. God is always ready to show Himself true in the lives of His children when they are readily obedient. This is through a variety of avenues and not only in the major ones like healing or living in divine health, but also in all areas of life. God will make everything, within His child's life, overly divine. The child will constantly soar like an eagle as is written in the Word. Our relationship with the God of power will cause us to flow in power. The good thing is this, that even if things don't seem good, God gives His obedient child a good reason why, gives grace to endure, patience and hope for a better outcome.

2 Samuel 5:10 And David went on, and grew great,
and the LORD God of hosts was with him.

Through a careful study of the Bible, several specific phrases should be drawn to one's attention. Some of these are, *"if you will," "if you don't," "obey me and I will"* or *"call onto me."* These phrases happen to appear a lot in the Old Testament. However, it isn't the number of times that these phrases appear that I desire to focus upon. I desire to dwell on what came about when these statements were, either obeyed or disobeyed, by the children of Israel. Every time God used these phrases, He actually brought into force a new dimension to the kind of relationship He desired to have with His people. Jesus Himself first left us instructions and thereafter, sent us the Teacher whose duty is to ensure that we follow these instructions properly.

Let us put into context, as done earlier on, in this paragraph, a few of the phrases that Christ Himself used. Jesus Christ said that, *"If ye love me, keep my commandments"* also *"If ye abide in me, and my words abide in you."* Later, in 1 John 3:23-24, John writes that we love Him when we obey His instructions *(commands)*. The aspect of love within our relationship with God is brought into focus herein. Our love for God is proven through our hunger and drive to obey His instructions.

1John 3:23-24 And this is his commandment, That we should believe
on the name of his Son Jesus Christ, and love one another, as he
gave us commandment. And he that keepeth his commandments
dwelleth in him, and he in him. And hereby we know that he
abideth in us, by the Spirit which he hath given us.

In this topic; *The basis of our relationship;* I need us to first grasp the concept, that our relationship is also based on a family setup. That God, the Creator of all, plays the role of a Father and we, that are believers in His Son Christ Jesus, play the role of children. In this, I am not talking about God as God (Sovereign ruler) but as God, a parent. It's not about Him being the God who rules the earth and can clear His enemies in the twinkling of an eye. I am talking about Him as the ideal family man. This abolishes the belief that He is far away in Heaven, too foreign to us or His ways too high for us anymore. This eliminates the false humility that states we are not worthy, brought on by ignorance. We were once not worthy of Him but Jesus Christ lovingly cleansed us of our sins reconciling us to Him. We are now part of His family and not visitors in His household.

We should have understood by now that this relationship isn't man-made or human-designed. It hasn't come into force through haggling in any boardroom or any kind of brokerage deals. This relationship came into force through a particularly glorious event. This event isn't, as many may think, the Cross at Calvary and surely not when Jesus Christ resurrected from the dead. It didn't start at the time we heard about Jesus Christ; but rather when, we <u>accepted</u> Him.

The day we acknowledged that all that we have been told about Him is true and believed *Romans 10:8-9*. That is when this relationship, though having been preordained before the foundations of the world were formed, came into force. It was after this procedure that you and I could call God, Father and He could call us, sons and daughters in response. We therefore have, indeed and without question, already crossed that great chasm that had separated us from God, with our faith in Jesus Christ being the enabling power. *(This is a reminder).*

Where do instructions come in herein? This is a most crucial question.

If you have been keen so far, I safely believe that you have now understood that instructions are different from orders. They are keys to some particular doors; they are the channel through which the good from God flows into our lives. The preliminary thing that God does, when having people believe in Jesus Christ is; He gives them the ability (*The quality of being able to perform; a quality that permits or facilitates achievement or accomplishment*) to accept His instructions. He gives us the grace for obedience, removing all the elements of rebelliousness.

God says this; that if you will believe in His report about Christ, then shall you be His child and shall also attain eternal Life. *If you believe.* This may as well be translated as, *if you accept and agree with me about what I have told you (God speaking).* Instructions are the key to the new birth and living as a new person as noted herein. *Colossians 1:12-13. Giving thanks unto the Father, which hath made us meet to be partakers of the inheritance of the saints in light: Who hath delivered us from the power of darkness, and hath translated us into the kingdom of his dear Son:*

The state of being disobedience or rather, not following an instruction makes God's wrath come upon one but obedience causes us to have favor with Him. Interestingly, most of us are obedient in one area but disobedience in another. For example, one can be obedient in tithing but disobedient in letting go of the past. I oppose the school of thought that God, as God, has no emotiveness. He does have emotions just as we do. He does laugh *(if and when happy)*, He does grieve *(due to sinfulness)* and He does feel remorse too just as we do. When He says that He is pleased with you, it is similar to when you are with someone you love and are happy to be with that someone. That big genuine smile that you put on is what is upon our Father's face, shining upon His obedient child.

Being disobedient may not push you out of the family of God but it limits or hampers the flow of God's power. I don't believe that God is in the business of saving then dumping. But an obedient child can't be equally favoured with a disobedient one. The grace overflows in the obedient one's life compared to the other. Disobedience is also another form of unbelief in God though He has already proven Himself to be true and faithful. This is the kind of child Israel was during the time in the wilderness. Regardless of all the mighty deeds of God; they still complained and succumbed to fear at the sight of any little challenge.

John 3:16 For God so loved the world, that he gave his only begotten Son, that <u>whosoever believeth</u> in him should not perish, but have everlasting life.

10. KEYS FOR DOORS OPENING

*Malachi 3:10 Bring ye all the tithes into the storehouse, that there may
be meat in mine house, and prove me now herewith, saith the LORD
of hosts, if I will not <u>open you the windows</u> of heaven, and pour you
out a blessing, that there shall not be room enough to receive it.*

*Isaiah 26:2 <u>Open ye the gates,</u> that the righteous
nation which <u>keepeth the truth</u> may enter in.*

In my Salvation life, I have listened to quite a good number of
sermons and read a number of books which deal with the issue of
attaining breakthroughs in finances or any other areas. These materials
aim at propelling readers or listeners into new realms concerning
their individual needs; which is a right and proper thing. Some of the
mainstream systems are through the wisdom of seed sowing, fasting,
favour declarations amongst various others. These are indeed ingredients
for a successful life in God.

However, we should understand that these are all offshoots of the
standard system of acquiring the blessings of God. The Word of God
is the stem from which all others protrude as stems. All these other
methods that we may choose to use are simply prophetic channels of
the Word of God. We must understand that everything that we seek
to establish or have established in our lives has to be sourced from the
Word of God. Anytime you sow seed or give according to the scripture,
you are guaranteed to receive or experience your harvest as the resultant
action of your action. Nevertheless, after obeying the Word of God,
the question arises; how does God get us to acquire this fulfillment of
scripture?

In answer to the above question, I carried out some research involving the patient study and re-studying of the lives of God's people, in the Bible, who walked in divine blessings. This was about the people who actually experienced the faithfulness of God in their lives. They did experience the practical blessings that God had promised them. I wasn't looking for people that gained through straining but those who gained *without* much of human efforts. Achievement of much through grace, not sweat. Examples of these are Abraham, Jacob, Isaac, David the king amongst the many others and this list can include your name too. It was after this study that I discovered a key, by the revelation of the Holy Spirit, to the unlocking the floodgates of heaven in one's life.

We must all, as Christians, understand that it is our prophetic right to be blessed. However, many a Christian do miss out much of these blessings due to a variety of reasons. Some self created and others due to other peoples acts or choices e.g. parents. We need to combine other essential tools with prayer and fasting. When this is done, we shall be able to turn our lives around in a remarkable way. All these keys will be important in the process of birthing our spiritual blessings from the heavenly realms and into the physical. *Ephesians 1:3 Blessed be the God and Father of our Lord Jesus Christ, who hath blessed us with all spiritual blessings in heavenly places in Christ*

In the quoted Malachi verse, that commenced this topic, God says He will open the floodgates of heaven. This means that, that there are things for you contained in the heavenly realms which you will need to access from the physical plane we exist on. Since you currently exist within the physical plane, you will have to reach out to them spiritually in order to possess them then manifest them physically, on earth. A spiritual procedure of tithing done physically and has spiritual reactions manifesting physically.

I realized that the receiving of these blessings was always preceded by a specific instruction or set of instructions. Everything which was still in the promise status came into the tangible and usable stage after the instruction was implemented. All those who experienced the fulfillment of God's promises had to first obey God prior and not thereafter. The more instructions that were carried out dutifully, the more the blessings the obedient one experienced. God, in *Malachi 3:10*, clearly shows us that the doors are only to be opened after something was done; the instructions contained in the process of tithing had to be carried out. Since God's Word doesn't change or expire, if you obey such, then you can claim the door to be opened and it shall be opened.

However, you might be amongst those who say I have done that but seen nothing yet. I don't purport to speak over your situation but there is a general negligence of the issue of receiving from God. Many don't prepare to receive as a right. They believe that they will receive only if it's God's will. Tithe as you prepare a place for the blessings to land upon for God isn't a careless rewarder. He is a diligent steward of resources.

Keenly listen (*by faith of course*) to what God told the children of Israel before giving them the land He promised them. We should understand that Abraham had already set foot upon that land centuries before then. That's the land that God took him round stating that He has given it to his descendants. God said......

Deuteronomy 28:1-2 And it shall come to pass, if thou shalt hearken diligently unto the voice of the LORD thy God, to observe and to do all his commandments which I command thee this day, that the LORD thy God will set thee on high above all nations of the earth: And all these blessings shall come on thee, and overtake thee, if thou shalt hearken unto the voice of the LORD thy God.

We can note that they were already prophetically blessed even when in slavery in Egypt. God who never lies had decreed His blessing them as a promise to Abraham His servant and friend. There was, however, a major requirement to be first met by them before their entering this prosperity. This requirement was; the absolute obedience to His instructions. I wonder what instruction God has given you today that you are yet to diligently follow? Instructions are more than just plain law or orders. Obedience to the Law of God, though mandatory, should be done within the atmosphere of grace.

Divine ideas are also included within instructions or simply go hand in hand. These are concepts formulated in God's mind not on earth. An idea from God is a power-packed guidance tool that will make your performance distinct.

Divine ideas are received as instructions after building a strong relationship with the God of all provision. The specific instruction He gives you will be your key to unlocking your doors of blessings. I have discovered that many Christians pray for hours on end, they fast for numerous days yet remain the same. I was in the same position a while back when starting off the youth ministry at church. I prayed extremely hard which wasn't wrong but my breakthrough came through when I asked God for a divine idea *(instruction)* through which success would flow. He deposited one in my heart and that changed everything.

God's instructions for the hour will get your business up and progressive better than ever. His power will work effectively in you. *Ephesians 3:20 Now unto him that is able to do exceeding abundantly above all that we ask or think, according to the power that worketh in us.* A door's lock will only function in response to its specific key. The key to Salvation is the name of Christ Jesus. There are many locked outside of Salvation.

You have obeyed the Word of God, thereby forming a strong relationship with Him; now you may ask Him for that divine instruction or rather, key, through which you will open the door.

Let me mention how these keys *(also called divine ideas)* help us. Though Abraham was a God fearing man of faith he needed the key of animal husbandry to prosper. It was actually through animal rearing that he prospered. Isaac was a farmer and herdsman too. At one time, while famine was being experienced and many were running away for solace in Egypt; he was cautioned by God not to leave but instead, was instructed to plant. He did reap a hundredfold that season regardless of the prevailing climatic conditions.

Had he disobeyed that instruction, because it seemed unorthodox; he would have failed in his endeavours despite being the promised child. Apostle Paul was a fiery evangelist who started off his ministry struggling with the Jews. However, he experienced his breakthrough in ministry when he obeyed the instruction to go work amongst the gentiles. This was his true area of calling. An instruction borne out of prayer pushed him into his destiny.

All these men, however anointed, were born of a woman as we all were. They needed to be transformed by the Holy Spirit just as we also are. This proves that you too can succeed, as they did, through obedience to instructions from God. Remember that He isn't a respecter of men; He simply recognises the obedient ones.

Acts 13:46-49 Then Paul and Barnabas waxed bold, and said, It was necessary that the word of God should first have been spoken to you: but seeing ye put it from you, and judge yourselves unworthy of everlasting life, lo, we turn to the Gentiles. For so hath the <u>Lord commanded us, saying, I have set thee to be a light of the Gentiles,</u> that thou shouldest be for salvation unto the ends of the earth. And when the Gentiles heard this, they were glad, and glorified the word of the Lord: and as many as were ordained to eternal life believed. And the word of the Lord was published throughout all the region.

Romans 11:13 For I speak to you Gentiles, inasmuch as I am the apostle of the Gentiles, I magnify mine office:

Why is an instruction so important?

It's important because God will readily back it compared to things which we just want Him to do for us. His instructions in your life will also effect good, positive changes in other people's lives. If you ask God to give you a way forward, and He does, you will surely have success for it's His mind working for you. This is how you will easily and efficiently overcome that demonic bondage or embargo over your life for good. Another name for this kind of instruction is; a **REVELATION** (*Communication of knowledge to man by a divine or supernatural agency*). It is a system that is beyond the confines of logic.

On the other hand, disobedience will always result in devastating failures. This could be much earlier or much later in the life of the disobedient person. The worst experience is the reaping of the fruits of disobedience late in life wherein the chances of correcting your wrongs are minimal. Saul the king had clearly been instructed to wait for Prophet Samuel but he got too restless. Fear overwhelmed him such that he became too fearful of the situation to obey God. Fear has been the major adversary to obedience to instructions. The instruction was; wait. This was regardless of whether the men were deserting his camp or the philistines had come upon him. Fear and trust in men cost him the kingdom.

Sometimes, instructions can sound very simple, easy to brush off. However, the results, whether in obedience or disobedience are far from simple. Moses at Meribah was instructed by God to toss a stick into the bitter water to turn it sweet. He did it, getting the right and desired results. It wouldn't have been the same if he had failed to follow the instruction. Failure would have been his share. This is what happened when he struck the rock instead of speaking to it; disobedience is the breaking of the faith. It is an honour from God to get instructions from Him; He deserves to be obeyed.

11. FOR THE FULL USAGE OF RESOURCES

2 Kings 4:1 Now there cried a certain woman of the wives of the sons of the prophets unto Elisha, saying, Thy servant my husband is dead; and thou knowest that thy servant did fear the LORD: and the creditor is come to take unto him my two sons to be bondmen. And Elisha said unto her, What shall I do for thee? tell me, what hast thou in the house? And she said, Thine handmaid hath not any thing in the house, save a pot of oil.

A resource is that which enables or facilitates one in the quest to achieve an intended purpose. It may range from a simple tool, material to money or investment partners but the bottom line is; that it is a necessary facilitator.

As I shopped around the market from time to time, I took note that there wasn't any equipment that was be released into the market without its formal instruction manual. The equipment users don't look into the manual because the manufacturers considered them as idiots, but rather, because they needed their users to experience the equipment's full potential. The more you comprehend something's operative systems, the more you shall accomplish using it. In other words, the following of instructions is what will enable you to get your money's worth.

The widow in the above quoted scripture had an economic and family crisis just like many people have today. She may as well have been worse off in debt more than most people are today. She had no clue on how to solve the problem by herself but I thank God that she undertook the best, most sensible action; run to the man of God. I do believe that this may be the safest step to take for any believer, for in God's anointed men are good and godly solutions. His servants, that fear Him, will always have His wisdom that will always surpass the challenge at hand. It's about consulting those who stand in the council of the Lord.

Jeremiah 23:18 For who hath stood in the counsel of the LORD, and hath perceived and heard his word? who hath marked his word, and heard it?

Isaiah 50:4 The Lord GOD hath given me the tongue of the learned, that I should know how to speak a word in season to him that is weary: he wakeneth morning by morning, he wakeneth mine ear to hear as the learned.

I now need us to focus more, on the desperate woman than on the prophet. This is the situation that is pointed out to us, that she was in trouble and time had actually run out. She had totally panicked and would do anything that seemed helpful or necessary just to rid her and her children of the problem that was hovering over their heads. Now shift your attention to the method that the man of God utilized to help her. Do notice that he didn't simply start casting out demons of debt, as many Christians desire done today. This shouldn't be misconstrued to mean that demons can't or don't influence people's debt situations; because there are many instances in which they are the catalysts of the debts. There are demonic systems which do hold people in a prison-like state of debts. The true cure of such isn't in a financial seminar but deliverance.

The man of God simply asked her what she had; that which she still had within her control. He was actually pointing out to her that she can solve her financial problems using resources that she already had, when backed by the power in the anointing of God. This also confirms that God will never give you any challenge that will be too overwhelming for you. Furthermore, He has the guaranteed tendency to always make a way out for us.

How many Christians, around the world rush to get loans for business capital, before consulting or agreeing with God on the issue first? How many want or plan to get employment first and then save some money from their salaries so that they can start a business? Multitudes, is the answer!!!! Same as many Christians today, one of the reasons why she had remained locked down in debt was because she didn't know how to maximize on the potential in the resources that she had. Well, how would she have thought about that in her state of mind? Nice question; which I do answer with another question: why do we raise our eyes to

Him? Our God is an expert in using faith the size of a mustard seed to move mountains. What is the comparison between a mustard seed and a mountain? None!! The debt wasn't the major issue; rather, it was the utilization of any and all resources available to her.

Now how did she unlock the potential in her overlooked "little oil" of a resource? The man of God gave her a simple instruction coupled with faith and it worked wonders beyond imagination. If you are instructed to sow a particular seed for your breakthrough, please do so without fretting. Don't ask about how will a little money avail school fees to me? It is about getting the Almighty involved in the situation. The widow of Zarepath was not simply awaiting death but was actually preparing for it. She had calculated how long after the little morsel of bread that she and her son would succumb to the famine. However, the story changed after she obeyed the instruction from the man of God. She took the flour as the seed, sowed it and reaped the harvest for three and a half years.

> *2 Kings 4:3-7 Then he said, Go, borrow thee vessels abroad of all thy neighbours, even empty vessels; borrow not a few. And when thou art come in, thou shalt shut the door upon thee and upon thy sons, and shalt pour out into all those vessels, and thou shalt set aside that which is full. So she went from him, and shut the door upon her and upon her sons, who brought the vessels to her; and she poured out. And it came to pass, when the vessels were full, that she said unto her son, Bring me yet a vessel. And he said unto her, There is not a vessel more. And the oil stayed. Then she came and told the man of God. And he said, Go, sell the oil, and pay thy debt, and live thou and thy children of the rest.*

Going back to the Elisha widow, she got aided in the utilizing of everything she had for her breakthrough. These resources were, her energy, the jars, her children's energy, ability to trade plus the once "little oil". A good instructor will make sure that the instructed should never waste any resources allocated to him or her. We increasingly need good instructors within the body of Christ who will help us utilize all the resources that God has already invested within us. These are the people that will not push us to ask for more until we have exhausted what we already have. If the man in the parable of the talents had an ear for instructions, I bet he would have also multiplied his one talent. Understand this, that that he already had the capacity within him to trade the talent for more.

How does a flask of oil get multiplied if it's not by power? The laws of physics and chemistry were defied therein. However, the power to multiply the oil was preceded by obedience to an instruction; disobedience to the instruction would have caused a non-miraculous situation. Disobedience can limit power as we have evidently seen. Disobedience is like an *access denied, stop* or *no through way* sign for power.

I always look back to this miraculous occurrence in the life of Jesus Christ; when He asked the disciples to feed the crowd but they couldn't see how. However, to Jesus Christ, the little fish and loaves of bread were resources enough because God was on His side. All that is needed is one with the right mindset and the power of God to back him up. These two items helped to transform the situation so tremendously such that we are still inspired by that miracle. God needed a man that believed in Him, His power activated through faith and people's willingness to obey the instructions issued. What if Jesus was disobedient to God? I dare not imagine what our story would have been today.

The instruction from the right person, given and obeyed at the right moment, will totally solve the problem that you are experiencing. We don't need to be borrowers to help ourselves; we first need to get into the position of being easily instructed, coupled with our faith in God and all will be well. If we allow the wisdom of God to manifest freely, there isn't a thing in this world that we cannot utilize for success in our lives.

12. THEY PRECEDE A NEW STAGE IN LIFE

1 Samuel 16:1....fill thine horn with oil, and go, I will send thee to Jesse the Bethlehemite: for I have provided me a king among his sons.

1 Samuel 16:13 Then Samuel took the horn of oil, and anointed him in the midst of his brethren: and the Spirit of the LORD came upon David from that day forward. So Samuel rose up, and went to Ramah.

At this point, I believe that it is proper to presume that it is now understood clear that the purpose(s) of an instruction isn't simply about; dos or don'ts. We have established that God's instructions are much deeper and far more complex than that. Furthermore, it is wise that we also realize that we are created to experience new things everyday in our lives. When I talk of new things; I am not insinuating that Salvation gets stale or comes into a place where it needs renewal. Salvation is a constant state, however, we are to keep progressing in it. We need to keep getting deeper and deeper into the Truth as it is revealed to us by the Holy Spirit. We have to keep unfolding the mystery that is Christ Jesus, discovering something more about our God, and that is the exciting thing about our God's infinite nature.

We aren't meant to simply stick to a particular conditioning for the rest of our lives in. Growth, naturally, is in different stages and paces. Let's use the natural birth process wherein a person is born totally helpless, wholesomely in need of the guardian's assistance. That child later outgrows its dependency on the mother or guardian, though it is still the same person and will remain the same person at old age. Even unto death. The humanity of this person never changes even for one bit but the person doesn't remain in the same physical, emotional or mental status all through his or her life. That person keeps developing in the different stages of life.

This is the same principle with the things of God. His children must grow into the new stages of their lives in Him. There are instructions that are given specifically for every stage in development and they do differ from each other. The instructions for raising a toddler are different from those for handling an adolescent. At a particular stage, old instructions are discarded for they have completed their purpose and new instructions are given for smooth transitioning and subsequently, the new stage in life. Growth is mandatory in God's design. Stagnation isn't on His agenda at all and instructions do serve as the bridges in the accomplishment of this purpose.

> *1 Corinthians 13:11 When I was a child, I spake as a child,*
> *I understood as a child, I thought as a child: but when*
> *I became a man, I put away childish things.*

Look at what God explains to us in chapter 6 of the book of Hebrews. He is advising us to use His divine instructions to help us grow into the next stage of lives and that some, due to lack of these relevant instructions, designate. Our lives are about progress for we are not made of still waters. Stagnation is literally the same as deadness. Running waters are mostly fresh unlike the still waters. Anytime a Christian's spiritual life remains stagnant, spiritual flies and frogs will find habitation in it for it has the conditions conducive for their festering.

> *Hebrews 6:1-3 Therefore leaving the principles of the doctrine of*
> *Christ, let us go on unto perfection; not laying again the foundation of*
> *repentance from dead works, and of faith toward God, Of the doctrine*
> *of baptisms, and of laying on of hands, and of resurrection of the dead,*
> *and of eternal judgment. And this will we do, if God permit.*

The writer of Hebrews is advising that we endeavour to acquire the teaching *(information and relevant application methods)* that will facilitate our growing into the next level or stage in our relationship with God. It's not about a new, smaller or greater kind of Salvation. He is simply concentrating on the saved person realizing that he or she MUST GROW in God. He desires that we gain more and cover larger spiritual territories. If we have been given any Spiritual gifts then we should understand them better and use them more efficiently.

If you are called to help the needy, then develop in it through understanding the heart of Christ, in giving to the needy. There is more beyond where you are right now. There is more beyond what you know right now. He emphasizes on approaching our Salvation as building a tower of many stories, you just have to keep going higher and higher until the purpose is attained; Salvation of our souls.

In referring to the earlier quoted verses, there are two classic examples of people who got into a new stage in their lives through obedience of instructions. Prophet Samuel is the common denominator in both lives. The two subjects of our study, David and Saul, were mere local boys. This remained so until they and Prophet Samuel obeyed an instruction concerning them. There was nothing significantly unique about them, neither did they aspire to have or be anyone great in the land. However, Prophet Samuel was called of God and instructed to anoint them at their specific God-appointed times; this is what changed their lives from shepherd boy and donkey searcher to kings in their respective timelines.

It is a fact that even our Lord Christ Jesus came into the world through the fulfillment of instructions. The result of this is the new kind of Life that we have today. This is the kind of Life which the men of old never understood and simply yearned to have a taste of it. Anytime you desire to step into a new level in life; simply ask the Holy Spirit for the necessary instructions concerning that place and obey them. He will cause you to enter the right door or apply for the right position, reducing your frustrations to zero.

13. GIVING OF TRUE LIGHT IN A DARK SITUATION

Psalms 119:105 Thy word is a lamp unto my feet, and a light unto my path.

Life in ministry has got me to understand that any Christian who keeps fluking solutions is a *simpleminded* Christian. This is a Christian who hasn't discovered who he or she really is. Dwelling in darkness isn't just about living in sin, it is also the state of a Christian being devoid of true guidance which is acquired from the Holy Spirit. This is when we are stuck and without direction, though we are not living in sin. It is true, that we do and regularly face tough situations many times in our lives which already predicted in God's Word.

Though sounding unexciting, these times are relevant to the establishment of our faith in Christ. There are times when we seem to be in deep darkness, such that we ask ourselves whether God is still with us or whether we are doing things all wrong. Other times, we may be in such bleakness that we just end up crying out of desperation and some do end up quitting. This is also where many decide to follow instructions with the *"let's see what happens"* kind of mindset; because they are too exasperated to carry out the instructions based on hope and faith.

Positive thinking isn't a priority any longer in this scenario. I have met many who simply drag themselves along because they don't want to "wrong" God by complaining about what they are going through. They fear, to anger God like the children of Israel in the desert.

I do comprehend this and it isn't criminal to experience a challenging situation, the problem truly lies in the next part; the, what you do in that situation, part. I have read in the scripture, of how the Israelites used to trouble Moses every time they experienced a dark period. They used to complain to Moses so much that they became oblivious of the fact that he too was in the same situation as they were *Numbers 11:5 We remember the fish, which we did eat in Egypt freely; the cucumbers, and the melons, and the leeks, and the onions, and the garlick: <u>But now our soul is dried away: there is nothing at all, beside this manna, before our eyes.</u>*

When they hungered he hungered too, when they got scared, he was also scared and even when they thirsted he thirsted too just as they did. They overlooked the fact that they were together at the same place and in the same conditions at all times. What distinguished Moses from the rest of the Israelites, was his willingness to turn to God and ask Him; "*Lord, what do you desire I do next?*" At Marah, *Exodus 15:23-24*, the people cried out because the water was bitter. They started thinking of how they would stone Moses because of the lack of fresh water; but he turned to God at that point and God showed him what to do.

As they murmured about onions, Moses on the other hand did what we should always do; ask for the directive of God that will bring us out of that problem. A directive that will take people out of the darkness that they are wondering about in. I studied in the book of *Acts Chapter 9* about Saul, when he was temporarily blinded. God instructed someone to give him back his sight. Prior to that, the men who were with him, by taking his hand and leading him to a safe place, did what instructions from God do for us in these tough situations. The instructions from our God will take you up from the lowest places and seat you at the highest places.

Acts 9:7-8 And the men which journeyed with him stood speechless, hearing a voice, but seeing no man. And Saul arose from the earth; and when his eyes were opened, he saw no man: but they led him by the hand, and brought him into Damascus.

Anytime we ask for God's help in Jesus name; when we are experiencing a solutions draught, God sends an instruction to hold our hand and bring us into a safe place. His desired place. There is no Christian who has the right to lack solutions. There shouldn't be a Christian that can dare to say that, "*I don't know what to do.*" We remain in such circumstances because we don't ask for solutions from God, which will normally be availed through instructions.

Exodus 17:4-6 And Moses cried unto the LORD, saying, <u>What shall I do</u>
<u>unto this people?</u> they be almost ready to stone me. <u>And the LORD said</u>
<u>unto Moses</u>, Go on before the people, and take with thee of the elders of
Israel; and thy rod, wherewith thou smotest the river, take in thine hand,
and go. Behold, I will stand before thee there upon the rock in Horeb; and
thou shalt smite the rock, and there shall come water out of it, that the
people may drink. And Moses did so in the sight of the elders of Israel.

When the Israelites cried that the water was bitter, Moses had no
power by himself to solve the problem. He however did what he knew
best; turning to God. God is always faithful to answer those who ask
Him for He knows that they trust in Him and He will not disappoint
them. It is important to note that Christ came as the Light of the world.
This was so that people would see Him and find the true solution and
free themselves from the shackles of darkness; Salvation through faith
in Him. God Himself brought us eternal Light to destroy the darkness
of death, but the only way through which Jesus will get you out of this
and any other kinds of darkness, is through the following of instructions
from Our Father. It is through instructions that we access the power
to destroy death (*demons, diseases, failures etc*) confirming what Christ
already did for us.

Hebrews 2:14 Forasmuch then as the children are partakers of flesh and
blood, he also himself likewise took part of the same; that through death
he might destroy him that had the power of death, that is, the devil;

Psalms 78:70-72 He chose David also his servant, and took him from the
sheepfolds: From following the ewes great with young he brought him to
feed Jacob his people, and Israel his inheritance. So he fed them according to
the integrity of his heart; and guided them by the skilfulness of his hands.

David is accredited in the psalm above, with the leading of Israel
with skillful hands and integrity of heart. These, (*integrity of heart and*
skillfulness of hands) he could only acquire through following the Word
of God as an obedient man, one that was always asking for instructions
on how to implement the Word. Paul the Apostle, shared David's key to

this kind of victorious living when giving instructions to Timothy his spiritual son. These were instructions not just for righteous living, as a person only, but to give understanding on how to handle the problematic situations at the church he was leading too.

There were instructions in Paul's letter, on how the young man could handle all the church sections including the older generation. Timothy was having a hard time and if I am right, he may have thought of quitting severally, atleast I know that I have considered that many times over. Spiritual work can be extremely hectic, placing an immense strain upon a person. However, he got encouraged and strengthened through the acquisition of instructions. Isn't it amazing that a young man in his thirties can lead even the oldest of people through obedience to instructions? Instructions from the Holy Spirit are superior to age or any other barriers.

It isn't proper for you, a child of God, to speak in *"I just don't know what to do"* kind of language. This isn't the way in the Christian family. One should simply say this *"Lord, what do you desire me to do?"*

14. THEY SET ONE APART FOR PURPOSE

Acts 13:1-3 Now there were in the church that was at Antioch certain prophets and teachers; as Barnabas, and Simeon that was called Niger, and Lucius of Cyrene, and Manaen, which had been brought up with Herod the tetrarch, and Saul. As they ministered to the Lord, and fasted, <u>the Holy Ghost said, Separate me Barnabas and Saul for the work whereunto I have called them</u>. And when they had fasted and prayed, and laid their hands on them, they sent them away.

From the above verses, there are several key pointers that are brought to light. These are vital in the corporate affairs of any church and through which God is able to influence one's life. Also in lieu of the fact that there are times that God desires public prayers and not closet prayers.

The pointers from this scenario are that; a) all the persons praying were believers. This doesn't simply mean the state of being saved but rather, the state of living in faith and by faith. The actual knowledge, that God is with you expressed through the expectancy of answers after prayer. b) The praying in unity; total teamwork in spiritual matters. They had overcome the spirit of discord which distorts peoples' intentions causing grief unto the Holy Spirit. They had purpose that was propelled in oneness. Corporate or group prayers must have this ingredient in order to be effective. c) Attentiveness to the Holy Spirit (*most important of all*). Why pray without knowledge of how to identify the voice of the Holy Spirit? We must understand that God will answer and wait upon Him keenly.

The plans that the Lord had for them particularly Paul and Barnabas were unknown to them. All they knew was that the Lord would answer them and give them directions in accordance to His loving will. Notice why it is always vital to afford the Holy Spirit His time to speak freely?

Don't muzzle Him in the name of long prayers but have fellowship (*an association of people who share common beliefs or activities*). It was within this mood of prayer that the Holy Spirit decided to reveal God's precreation plans to them *Ephesians 1:4 According as he hath <u>chosen us in him before the foundation of the world</u>...* He singled out Apostles Paul and Barnabas for a particular task.

Though there is so much work to do in the harvest fields of our God, He's never been a God of confusion with His workers running helter-skelter. With God, it's not a matter of anyone working anywhere at anytime because he or she is Spirit-filled. I have met many people who proudly say this, "*as for me, I got no issue with work/ministry, just place me anywhere*". Though sounding good, it is most pitiful and retrogressive. A jack of all trades is always a master of none. When Apostle Paul said that he could do all things through faith in Christ Jesus; he didn't mean anything or everything in the kingdom, but all that pertains to the duties assigned to him.

We do understand that there were times that he needed someone else to work with him. He needed Timothy in Corinth and Titus in Crete when he was in Rome. The body of Christ is about all of us doing our part in unison towards a common end; glorifying God through making sheep of many. There are, of course, particular times wherein we are needed to help another carry his or her cross, but this doesn't make it yours. None of us has been given two crosses to carry but to help each other according to the grace given us.

1Corinthians 12:25 That there should be no schism in the body; but that the members should have the same care one for another.

In the above verse *Acts 13:1-3*, we can clearly notice, how instructions come into play when God wants His work done. In the previous topic we also saw the use of instructions for confirmation; but in this topic, they reveal God's plans or purpose. It's great to see how many things instructions are and can be used to bring into reality. We did discover, that the brethren praying didn't know what God had planned. They were simply having a wonderful, Spirit-controlled time of prayer and waiting upon God. Paul and Barnabas already knew that they were called to preach the Gospel, but if the Holy Ghost didn't tell them what He exactly purposed, they and the others wouldn't have known that it was time to leave the group for the different assignment. How many times or days have you spent doing something right somewhere wrong?

We do further understand that the Holy Spirit didn't say what they were going to do, in this verse, He simply said there was work to be done and ordered the separation. The brethren obeyed the instruction by blessing the two and releasing them. When God has a purpose for you, He will first give the instruction. This instruction will be the guiding tool on how you are to prepare for that purpose. The others' laying hands on them, showed that they acknowledged that, God had different plans for the two, apart or away from them.

One major issue that we should all relate well with is that though we have one God, one Spirit or one Mediator, but diverse mandates. My mandate isn't your mandate and vice versa. This is why Apostle Paul taught concerning the different parts of the same body working towards the same end. So what sets us apart? It is the designate duties that we are instructed to carry out. A person without his specific instructions from God about his purpose is a person that is failing in the body of Christ. You must know what God has specifically set you apart for and this is only through the knowledge of His instructions for you. Though we must support each other; we can't do the other's share of work and that's why we are one in Spirit but endowed with different capacities.

1 Corinthians 12:11 But all these worketh that one and the selfsame Spirit, dividing to every man severally as he will.

In this paragraph, I will use Prophet Jeremiah as the example. I desire to look deeper into his ministry as a prophet. In order for us to do this effectively, we will also have to focus on how he started. Prior to God calling him, Jeremiah was simply a priest. It wasn't that meeting with God that made him one for he was already executing his priestly duties at Anathoth, *Jeremiah 1:1 The words of Jeremiah the son of Hilkiah, of the priests that were in Anathoth in the land of Benjamin.* According to normalcy, he would live as a priest and leave this world as a priest: but God originally had a different purpose for him.

So what is the special point herein? The first result of the instructions from God was his separation from the rest of the priests, *Jeremiah 1:5 ..., and I ordained thee a prophet unto the nations.* God first set him apart then gave him his true purpose. God had the purpose of destroying kingdoms while planting others but He needed someone tailor-made by Him, for that purpose. As unique as this purpose was, without instructions from God, it would not have been realised. Though you are as strong and as unique as your obedience to instructions is, you are also as weak as your ignorance of the instructions of God for your life is.

The stronger the ignorance, the weaker you are; the more the knowledge and obedience, the stronger you are. His instructions from God gave him rights to minister as the spokesman of God and not the simple offering of incense at the sanctuary. Purpose is specific and it's only through the instructions of God that one will be separated from the rest for such. This also gives us the understanding that instructions can be unique as to a specific person just as they can be for a large group of people.

Jeremiah 1:6-7 Then said I, Ah, Lord GOD! behold, I cannot speak: for I am a child. But the LORD said unto me, Say not, I am a child: for thou shalt go to all that I shall send thee, and whatsoever I command thee thou shalt speak.

When you have received, understand and start implementing your instructions from God, there is nothing that can stop you. No demon or situation can stop you at all. You may face opposition, which is good, but not being stopped. It's only you that can stop yourself through callousness, laxity, ignorance or pride. You will carry out business successfully when you get specific instructions on how to conduct it, for God will supercharge you beyond your peers and competitors. Instructions from God come with the relevant power packages for your successful operation. His instructions will make you do business so uniquely such that you won't need to mimic others. His purpose for you is that you carryout business with a kingdom mentality.

15. TO FULFILL ALL RIGHTEOUSNESS

Mathew 3:15-16 And Jesus answering said unto him, Suffer it to be so now: for thus it becometh us to fulfil all righteousness. Then he suffered him. And Jesus, when he was baptized, went up straightway out of the water: and, lo, the heavens were opened unto him, and he saw the Spirit of God descending like a dove, and lighting upon him:

Righteousness is a system that is brought about through the carrying out of the Word of God. It isn't, simply, the act of calling on God and having faith that He will respond. Righteousness is the total lifestyle of a person who has been made holy through the ever precious cleansing Blood of Jesus Christ. There is absolutely none that can be holy unless washed by the blood of Jesus. Righteousness, however, is the practicing of faith; this is what is effected by the God-fearing person who has been made holy. Do know that one may fear God but still not be holy. There are many who respect God but the blood of Jesus Christ hasn't worked anything in their lives. Righteousness may have a long list of definitions but I choose to summarize it as joyfully doing God's will here on earth as it is in heaven.

John the Baptist knew that, Jesus Christ was far greater than him and naturally desired to humble himself during the baptism section. However, obedience to the Word of God is what was needed and not just the simple, humility that he desired to exercise. God didn't need that style of humility; He simply desired His will to be done. We have to function under the prompting of the Holy Spirit and not the simple canonical knowledge that we have inherited from men. Jesus, in regard to His being baptized by John, personally used the statement; *to fulfill all righteousness.* This is because John baptizing Him and not Him baptizing John was an instruction of God the Father. It was a strategic step instructed by God Himself.

It was obvious to God that Jesus Christ was greater than John the Baptist, but His decision was above John's logic. All righteousness means that all things are reconciled to God in Christ Jesus through obedience. It also means that our actions are in line with what He wants and not what we think is right. It is through Christ that we are enabled to do goodly actions. Through this act of baptism, by one less than Him, we received a new life. The Spirit wouldn't rest upon us if John disobeyed in the name of humility. Every time we follow instructions, we indeed do fulfill all righteousness unlike when we don't. There are times we did things because they seem good to us and believed it was what God wanted.

The fulfilling of all righteousness is also the action of bringing God's truth or desire into reality. This is when what God has desired done is done by His people. Righteousness is very specific and not vague as many take it to be. Jesus ushered us into the royal priesthood through which we are also the light of the world. If the world is receiving light from another source besides us, then we are not fulfilling all righteousness. If the witchdoctors or scientists are providing more solutions than the church, then all righteousness isn't being fulfilled. Jesus instructed that we are to produce solutions for the whole of the human race and creation in general. That He would draw men of many nations to our lights. It is we who are in Christ that the whole of creation is waiting upon and not any other person. This is why people have gone even to the extent of waiting for aliens to come from outer space yet the name of Jesus is the source of all answers. Why do heathen music, shows, movies and other satanic projects keep swaying even the children of the believers away from the truth and into darkness? This is because we aren't fulfilling all righteousness.

Romans 8:19-22 For the earnest expectation of the creature waiteth for the manifestation of the sons of God. For the creature was made subject to vanity, not willingly, but by reason of him who hath subjected the same in hope, Because the creature itself also shall be delivered from the bondage of corruption into the glorious liberty of the children of God. For we know that the whole creation groaneth and travaileth in pain together until now.

We must look around us today, as Christians and ask ourselves some questions like these. Who is the one handling the economies of the world? Who is providing the health care solutions for the whole world? Who is engaging warring parties in the signing of peace treaties? If in any of these areas, it isn't a child of God; then we are failing in fulfilling all righteousness. Don't say that God can use anything or anyone; why should He use anything yet you, who are royalty, are there? Righteousness isn't holiness, it is the status of performing or exercising the Word of God as it should be within your holy nature.

This is when we ensure that everything runs in accordance with what the Word of God has decreed about it. This is about all areas of life e.g. healing, finances, family, faith etc. This is walking by faith and not by sight. Why should your flocks experience barrenness yet God promised that if we obey Him barrenness won't exist amongst us? Jesus asked John the Baptist to stop trying to wrongly humble himself and just do what God had ordained to be done. Thus, the lesser one baptized the greater one for the greater came as a servant not as a master. This was God's will.

Many talk a lot about the God who answers by fire. They talk it over and over again, but it is rare for many to see its actualization in their lives. I have personally witnessed God answer by *fire* severally in my life over the years. There is the very unique statement that Prophet Elijah made which many have always overlooked. Let's go into the Word and read it for ourselves;

1 Kings 18:36-38 And it came to pass at the time of the offering of the evening sacrifice, that Elijah the prophet came near, and said, LORD God of Abraham, Isaac, and of Israel, let it be known this day that thou art God in Israel, and that I am thy servant, and that I have done all these things at thy word. Hear me, O LORD, hear me, that this people may know that thou art the LORD God, and that thou hast turned their heart back again. Then the fire of the LORD fell, and consumed the burnt sacrifice, and the wood, and the stones, and the dust, and licked up the water that was in the trench.

The situation at that time was a pretty dark one. Idolatry had become so great such that Elijah was afraid that the people would soon forget their maker. Good priests at that time were a scarce commodity. Through this Bible passage, we do realize that God didn't simply give His answer to Elijah, a man, but to Elijah, an executer of His instructions. God simply confirmed the righteousness that Elijah the prophet had exhibited. We must comprehend how God relates with His servants. He endows them with the ability to do good generally and to perform what pleases Him. Elijah's obedience to instructions as a servant pleased God causing Him to restore Israel unto righteousness. Righteous deeds do indeed please God for it means that the doer is upholding his testimony of God acquired through faith in Christ Jesus.

Furthermore, fulfilling all righteousness is also the using of the right systems allocated by God for the proper achievement of results. At one time, Moses was instructed by God to speak to the rock but he hit it. Though the results were the same, for water still flowed out, the trigger was the wrong one. He had disobeyed. How many times do you get the desired results though you used the wrong system? This is also what is called *breaking faith*. It means that the system God chose for that purpose has been dropped for another which He didn't choose. Out of His good measure of mercy, He may answer relevantly, but He will not overlook your disobedience. If God were not as merciful and loving as He is, we would all not be alive today.

God has given us instructions so that we can do things as He wants them done and for that, He will reward us. Follow them and His power will be made available to you in abundance. Ignorance has to come to end in our lives and that we should now start winning knowledgeably. Do right, live right.

*Acts 17:30 And the times of this ignorance God winked at;
but now commandeth all men every where to repent:*

16. TO FULFILL PROPHECY

Mathew 1:22,23 Now all this was done, that it might be fulfilled which was spoken of the Lord by the prophet, saying, Behold, a virgin shall be with child, and shall bring forth a son, and they shall call his name Emmanuel, which being interpreted is, God with us.

For us Christians, prophecy (*a prediction; whether written or spoken*) is one of the most important avenues through which we connect with God and remaining within His will. God's plans are revealed to us through His servants as they are apportioned by the Holy Spirit through the gift of the word of wisdom. It is actually through prophecy that we are also assured of our faith in Christ. This is how we surely know what tomorrow has in store for our lives in the days to come and the inevitable eventualities in our lives. Furthermore, it is through prophecy that we are able to stand against anything that the devil throws at us or whatever challenges that may stand against us. This noble avenue, however, has been portrayed as controversial within the body of Christ and outside of it, with many so called prophets using manipulation or divination, duping believers for whatever personal gains they desire to achieve.

Now what role does or will an instruction play in the fulfillment of a prophecy we may ask? Shouldn't prophecy, if indeed so powerful, not birth itself or power itself into fulfillment? Can't God do it Himself or use His ever available angels without the need for any human involvement? After all, didn't He Create the heavens and the earth without any assistance from us? Yes, it's true that God doesn't need us, instead, He loves us; and furthermore, it's about what the Almighty God desires and this is what He has desired to use in the expression of His might. How will you know that He knows and designs the future if He doesn't speak it well before hand? Well, let me answer these questions in the next few paragraphs.

Firstly, let me emphatically state that any prophecy can only come into fulfillment through a specific instruction or chain of instructions. We must understand that a prophecy isn't just a prediction or an insight into the future but a reality that is in existence though yet to be experienced. It is yet to pass through our normal, human time and space. It is awaiting its specific, opportune time of enactment. Let us see some clear examples from the Word of God, which is the basis of our existence, through which we shall realise how prophecy works in conjunction with faith and instructions.

I learnt that, when the children of Israel were at the periphery of the Promised Land and prophecy was about to be fulfilled, God directed (instructed) them on what to do. Of course we know that they didn't do what God required of them due to fear and discouragement. The time for their inheritance prophecy's fulfillment had come, but they weren't obedient enough to birth it into reality.

> *Deuteronomy 1:20-21 And I said unto you, Ye are come unto the*
> *mountain of the Amorites, which the LORD our God doth give*
> *unto us. Behold, the LORD thy God hath set the land before*
> *thee: go up and possess it, as the LORD God of thy fathers*
> *hath said unto thee; fear not, neither be discouraged.*

Jacob's story is another example. He was given a prophetic word (*decree*) by his father Isaac in the name of a blessing. This is the same word which was confirmed by God on Jacob's way to his uncle Laban's place, Padan-Aram. We should not fail to notice that Jacob had left home with nothing but the clothes on his back and a vial of anointing oil. All he had to hold onto, concerning his future, was the blessing which contained the prophecy about what God would do for him in due season. That in the future, he would make him wealthy in all ways. God was going to fulfill the prophecy that was given to Abraham Jacob's life. As I noted earlier, prophecy is based on the gift of the word of wisdom. It is a fraction of what God shall do in the future, revealed to man through man.

Genesis 28:3-5 And God Almighty bless thee, and make thee fruitful, and multiply thee, that thou mayest be a multitude of people; And give thee the blessing of Abraham, to thee, and to thy seed with thee; that thou mayest inherit the land wherein thou art a stranger, which God gave unto Abraham. And Isaac sent away Jacob: and he went to Padanaram unto Laban

Another example is based on the return of the exiles and the rebuilding of the Temple in the time of Ezra. God's prophetic time for the return of the remnants and the rebuilding of the Temple had come. Though most of those that returned hadn't been in existence at the time of prophesying; this prophecy still stood. Now this is how it came to be fulfilled. God *instructed* King Cyrus to start it off of which he made the decree for the support of the Jews in this noble work. This is in line with what Isaiah prophesied in *Isaiah 44 and 45*. When the Jews who were with Ezra were questioned concerning what they were doing; they, in reply, told of God's prophecy concerning their actions. Instructions were the force behind this whole process as we can note.

Ezra 5:9 Then asked we those elders, and said unto them thus, Who commanded you to build this house, and to make up these walls?

Ezra 6:3 In the first year of Cyrus the king the same Cyrus the king made a decree concerning the house of God at Jerusalem, Let the house be builded, the place where they offered sacrifices, and let the foundations thereof be strongly laid; the height thereof threescore cubits, and the breadth thereof threescore cubits;

This prophecy, just as many others were, was implemented through the carrying out of instructions by obedient men regardless of their religious beliefs. The authority in a prophetic word is released through the implementation of instructions specifically tailored for it. Any duty that God gives to you, whether through His servants, a dream, a vision or any other mode of His choice, will be accomplished by you only through the application of the relevant guidelines. God guides and shows us how to do it. *Isaiah 28:26 For his God doth instruct him to discretion, and doth teach him.*

Many Christians do proclaim that the Abrahamic blessings are theirs and rightly so, *Galatians 3:29 And if ye be Christ's, then are ye Abraham's seed, and heirs according to the promise.* However, many live long in their lives without seeing what was prophetically decreed to be theirs. After toiling for some years, Jacob's prophetic time came; let's see what God instructed him to do so that he could be blessed tangibly thereby proving the prophesy true. The whole of Chapter 30, particularly from verse 32-41, simply shows him applying an instruction which was beyond the scope of human comprehension. Instructions can also come as divine ideas, as I noted in the earlier chapter.

> *Genesis 30:37-39 And Jacob took him rods of green poplar, and of the hazel and chesnut tree; and pilled white strakes in them, and made the white appear which was in the rods. And he set the rods which he had pilled before the flocks in the gutters in the watering troughs when the flocks came to drink, that they should conceive when they came to drink. And the flocks conceived before the rods, and brought forth cattle ringstraked, speckled, and spotted.*

Another example is Jesus Christ's time to come into this world through physical birth. Everything that had been prophesied about Him actually came into our physical, human realm through a set of obeyed instructions. His name and His protection from King Herod both came through instructions from God. Joseph and Mary only had to be obedient to the letter in order for the promised King to come to us and fulfill purpose.

Why didn't God just kill Herod instead of directing them to flee from him? Much as none of us can purport to fully speak for God, I do understand that God places human beings within His divine plans as co-workers with Him; so we do have our roles to play. Otherwise, there would be no reason for us to be His children.

> *Mathew 1:20- 22 But while he thought on these things, behold, the angel of the Lord appeared unto him in a dream, saying, Joseph, thou son of David, fear not to take unto thee Mary thy wife: for that which is conceived in her is of the Holy Ghost. And she shall bring forth a son, and thou <u>shalt call his name</u>*

*JESUS: for he shall save his people from their sins. Now all this was done,
that it might be fulfilled which was spoken of the Lord by the prophet, saying,*

There is a myriad of other examples that we won't look into right
now, but you can study and meditate on them at your own time.
Conclusively, every prophecy given to us from God will only come to
pass if we have the specific instructions for it. Instead of sweating much
through hard labour, why don't you just ask God for His instructions?
His instructions will enable you, prepare you and eventually get you
there. Every promise in the scripture will materialize in your life through
the obedient following instructions.

How do we acquire instructions?

17. THROUGH THE STUDYING OF SCRIPTURE

Luke 4:17-18 And there was delivered unto him the book of the prophet Esaias. And when he had opened the book, he found the place where it was written, The Spirit of the Lord is upon me, because he hath anointed me to preach the gospel to the poor; he hath sent me to heal the brokenhearted, to preach deliverance to the captives, and recovering of sight to the blind, to set at liberty them that are bruised,

Personally, I was full of joy as a Christian the day I discovered that I have been hearing from God very clearly. This was after a long period of beating myself down with many doubtful questions. I suffered a lot of confusion whenever I heard other Christians discussing how God kept talking to them, of how He was visiting and directing them personally. For a long period, I felt so low and pondered much whether He really was with me or these others were more special than I. other's testimonies about their personal encounters with God kind of rattled my faith. Actually, I did feel faithless.

I later realized, by the Holy Spirit's grace, that God had indeed been talking to me daily and more clearly than I had ever thought. The fundamentals of a Christian's relationship with God are contained within His Word, commonly known as the Holy Bible. It is from here that we develop other methods of hearing from Him as we grow in Him. Nothing comes from beyond what is written for us. Every miraculous act or prophetic tool e.g. mantles, are offshoots of the Word. The Word God is the fountain for all things which are of God for the believer.

I Corinthians 3:11 For other foundation can no man lay than that is laid, which is Jesus Christ.

The closer (more acquainted) with God people get, the more audible and tangible He becomes to them. He ceases to be *"far"* away. What do I mean by getting closer with God? It's simply this, that the more we obey Him, the stronger the connection He has with us because obedience creates a good relationship environment. How then do we obey Him? Though knowing what He wants or requires of us.

You can accomplish this through studying, meditation and doing that which is contained within His instructions manual; the Bible. There is a reason as to why the devil works round the clock to ensure that the believer doesn't read or rather, study the Word of God as efficiently as he or she should. He knows that without God's Word in us, we become susceptible to his doctrines. It is through this lack of studying the scripture that a person's relationship with God becomes detached.

Deuteronomy 11:18 Therefore shall ye lay up these my words in your heart and in your soul, and bind them for a sign upon your hand, that they may be as frontlets between your eyes.

It is in the Bible that we get all the fundamentals for a close and strong relationship with God. It is from here that we receive revelations concerning various situations. Isn't it interesting that though Christ was directly from God though through a woman's womb, the first thing He did was to read the instructions detailing the reasons for His existence from the written Word?

The Holy Spirit insisted to Habakkuk and Moses too about having the Word written on tablets. A hard copy of what both Moses and Habakkuk had received from Him. God insisted that the children of Israel write down the Laws He had given them together with the record of the mighty deeds He had accomplished for them. it is dangerous not to have the Word in you. In Judges 2, the Bible indicates that after Joshua's death, leaders who didn't know God or His deeds took over the leadership reins. It is these who started the idol worshiping in Israel; this was because they were empty of God by not indulging the Word of God.

They were to teach these and tell them to their children so that they too may have a good and strong relationship with Him. God was dealing with His written Word, the kind that anyone can access even without much prayer or fasting. Just visit the nearest bookshop and purchase your copy; that's how simple it is. You can even bless someone with a copy or it can even be borrowed.

Deuteronomy 11:18-19 Therefore shall ye lay up these my words in your heart and in your soul, and bind them for a sign upon your hand, that they may be as frontlets between your eyes. And ye shall teach them your children, speaking of them when thou sittest in thine house, and when thou walkest by the way, when thou liest down, and when thou risest up.

Habakkuk 2:2 And the LORD answered me, and said, Write the vision, and make it plain upon tables, that he may run that readeth it.

Prophecy and revelations are but for a time, but the Word is Eternal. The more you focus on the Word of God; the more God gets actively involved in your life. It is through His Word that we discover how to pray, heal the sick, cast out demons, fast, help the needy, forgive, walking in righteousness and all the rest. None of these is plucked from somewhere in the atmosphere; it is sourced from the Scripture.

Daniel was empowered to pray after reading the written prophesy concerning the restoration of the children of Israel. He knew right then, as an intercessor, what he was to do next. It was through this written Word of God that his assignment came up. Paul himself also had his assignment or instructions confirmed through the Scripture. The Scripture is God's mind set in written instructions since before the world was framed, revealing and explaining to us His nature in simplicity.

Isaiah 49:6 And he said, It is a light thing that thou shouldest be my servant to raise up the tribes of Jacob, and to restore the preserved of Israel: I will also give thee for a light to the Gentiles, that thou mayest be my salvation unto the end of the earth.

This was fulfilled in....

Acts 13:47-49 For so hath the Lord commanded us, saying, I have set thee to be a light of the Gentiles, that thou shouldest be for salvation unto the ends of the earth. And when the Gentiles heard this, they were glad, and glorified the word of the Lord: and as many as were ordained to eternal life believed. And the word of the Lord was published throughout all the region.

The Word is Jesus Christ and He has all power.

John 1:1-4 In the beginning was the Word, and the Word was with God, and the Word was God. The same was in the beginning with God. All things were made by him; and without him was not any thing made that was made. In him was life; and the life was the light of men.

18. SERVING UNDER AN OBEDIENT, INSTRUCTED PERSON

2 Kings 3:11 But Jehoshaphat said, Is there not here a prophet of the LORD, that we may enquire of the LORD by him? And one of the king of Israel's servants answered and said, Here is Elisha the son of Shaphat, <u>which poured water on the hands of Elijah</u>.

Mark 16:15-19 <u>And he said unto them, Go ye into all the world, and preach the gospel to every creature</u>. He that believeth and is baptized shall be saved; but he that believeth not shall be damned. And these signs shall follow them that believe; In my name shall they cast out devils; they shall speak with new tongues; They shall take up serpents; and if they drink any deadly thing, it shall not hurt them; they shall lay hands on the sick, and they shall recover. So then after the Lord had spoken unto them,

It was quite amazing to me, when I realized the importance of men in each other's lives concerning God's affairs. Noticeably, God has lots of times used one man to propel another into his or her intended destiny. He invests His commissioning authority to raise or anoint (empower) a man for his prophetic destiny within another man's custody. He believes that there is much He can do for one through another. It's not just about giving of instructions but also for guidance, protection and companionship too.

We should all, as God's children, understand that our God is a God of order and continuity. He has created a system where He sets others to start, then others to continue with the already commenced duty. He gave Adam ability to continue with the creation process that He Himself had already started. Everything in Adam's life was engineered to continue giving life even after his fall. This is the same system that we are functioning under even in the New Creation reality. It is the system of continuity, though this time, it is as sons of God and not of the old man; Adam. Adam did continue the process but under the system which had been corrupted by sinfulness. Jesus brought in the system which is devoid of decay for not even His flesh, in death, decayed in any way.

We do remember that instructions help one to avoid the wastage of time and resources. The time one would have used in order to gain information or learn the tools of a particular trade, is reduced through the process of following instructions. The one that ventured before the other and was successfully will educate the other on what he or she needs to know. Information that would have taken many years to acquire can be quickly acquired. Jesus Christ taught the disciples so much within a short span of time. They knew God and cultivated their obedience to Him through sitting under Jesus' wings. God desired men to know Him, as Christ did and this He accomplished by having one man instruct others.

Let me bring this to your attention, that we have mainly missed one very key detail in our lives. This is the issue of standing upon another's shoulders. It is a relay system of starting off from where another reached. You don't need to break fresh ground or start from scratch if you have one that went before you. You can take over the relay baton from the one who was just ahead or before you. It is important to understand that this is what enables us to see further and expand the inherited territories. You can only stand upon another's shoulders by obeying the instructions from that person. This is because, that very person is also a product of the obedient implementation of instructions. Obedience will link you with his or her spirit (anointing) smoothly.

1 Corinthians 3:10 According to the grace of God which is given unto me, as a wise masterbuilder, I have laid the foundation, and another buildeth thereon. But let every man take heed how he buildeth thereupon.

Here is a classic set of examples of great men who experienced much of God's power through this system. Samuel the great judge and prophet received instructions from Eli, Paul from Gamaliel, Titus from Paul, Solomon from King David, Esther from her uncle Mordecai, Ruth from Naomi her mother in-law; the list is quite long. On the other hand, Saul the king couldn't take simple instructions and we do know how his life came to its end. He basically had no instructor, he only turned to Samuel at the times of needs only. Instructions taking or receiving is the natural order of things in God's Kingdom. One receives them so that he or she, on the other hand, can pass them to another. This is a chain which can be only be broken through the disobedience of the receiving party.

Proverbs 4:1-4 Hear, ye children, the instruction of a father, and attend to know understanding. For I give you good doctrine, forsake ye not my law. For I was my father's son, tender and only beloved in the sight of my mother. He taught me also, and said unto me, Let thine heart retain my words: keep my commandments, and live.

Receiving of instructions from another, gives room for humility to operate, bringing in speedy growth. Wisdom is acquired through humility then cultivated over a period of time. Wisdom keeps the humble on the right track experiencing fewer mistakes in comparison to the arrogant ones. I do accept the fact that, regardless of our humility, we all do mistakes periodically and these do serve the purpose of teaching us. However, the arrogant will have a vein for blundering. They speak wrong, act wrong, pray amiss, everything about them is more of wrong than right. They are so messed up but they just can't seem to come round and recognize it. Saul the king was one such character; he even ended up going to a medium after God rejected him.

Instructions, if humble, will train one to produce good results. Such a person simply needs someone to take him or her under his or her wing and nurture him or her well. This will transform them from wrecks and into resourceful persons; people that are proactively malleable for the good of the body of Christ. This was also Christ's major quality. He was easy to guide by our Father in heaven, hence He completed His task successfully for our very own benefit. He talked about doing what He had learnt from the Father.

There is a major blessing that we acquire through this process. Getting instructions from another, gives the obedient one the opportunity to acquire all the grace (*unmerited favour*) that is functioning upon the instructing person's life. This is without having to break a sweat for it.

It is also known as the taping of mantles. God allows His grace that functions upon the instructor's life to flow onto his apprentice without the apprentice having to struggle, in prayer or otherwise, as much as the instructor may have done.

Through simple obedience and trust, Elisha received the double portion of what Elijah had just by asking for it. He didn't have to fast many days and nights for it. Joshua too, received the spirit of wisdom without even sacrificing anything much for it; all he needed was humility under Moses' tutorship. Timothy received his spiritual gift through the simple laying on of hands by Paul. All that Timothy needed to do to acquire the gift was to sit (*humble and obedient*) under and respect Apostle Paul's authority over his life.

This principle doesn't simply concern those in mainstream ministry i.e. pastors, deacons etc only. It also incorporates those within the corporate field. There isn't any competent manager that would desire to mentor or connect with a disobedient *mentee*. All progressive persons will seek to avoid these disobedient ones; ignorant characters who think they can simply outshine those who went before them. The fact that one has been successful in doing something over the years means that the upstart needs to listen to him and listening well he or she should. Obedience makes mentorship extremely easy and enjoyable for both the tutor or mentor and the one being tutored.

This kind grace can only come into existence, through the bond of obedience. This bond is in reality a sweat-free, power supply. God does recognize the role and authority of men over other men for He is the one who gives all authority. God wondered through Apostle John, how we can love Him whom we do not see yet love not they that we can see! It is the same thing within the spiritual principles of instructions. How can one be obedient to God, whom he doesn't see, yet be disobedient to God's servant whom he can see?

God has instituted a governance system where a man will always find himself in need to submit to another and another to submit to him too. This is a chain which, when broken, results in anarchy. It is the same in the heavens, angels answer to their superiors without sulking as many Christians or people generally do. There are angels that are under Archangel Gabriel's authority and same for Archangel Michael. When it was time for war in heaven it was Archangel Michael that led the troops in it *Revelation 12:7 And there was war in heaven: Michael and his angels fought against the dragon; and the dragon fought and his angels.* The term leading herein denotes obedience and submissiveness for without these ingredients there can be no leadership. Can the same be found in you?

Rebelliousness against this structure has been the cause of most of the problems in the world. Politicians don't respect their superiors and keep challenging them just for the sake of remaining "relevant", pastors not taking instructions because they think they are equal in anointing to their spiritual fathers, children literally disobeying their parents or teachers. This list is virtually endless and today, some laws that have been enacted today do actually support or propagate disobedience even towards God Almighty.

There are many people that started their businesses simply because they didn't want to be under instructions. They didn't start their own because they saw a market loophole that their products or services can handle, bettering the market in general. This is why there is a lot of undercutting and flooding of the market with mimicked services or products. Ingenuity isn't around much today. It is common for many employees to resign from their workplaces after learning the tools of trade only to start their own business using their former employer's clientele or customers.

This behavior is rampant within the fivefold ministry too. Many a pastor leave the church or ministry with part of the flock that they used to minister to in the name of the flock pursuing their anointing. This is absolute wickedness.

We should all learn to be humble and submissive to each other just as Christ submitted His Eternal glory to God and suffered as a man. God didn't forcefully humble Him, He instead, humbled Himself in order to serve God for our sakes. The greatest power system is the system of humility in love (*Agape*).

Philippians 2:7-8 But made himself of no reputation, and took upon him the form of a servant, and was made in the likeness of men: And being found in fashion as a man, he humbled himself, and became obedient unto death, even the death of the cross.

19. THROUGH ASKING GOD

1 Samuel 23:4 Then David enquired of the LORD yet again.
And the LORD answered him and said, Arise, go down to
Keilah; for I will deliver the Philistines into thine hand.

In the area of acquisition of instructions, this avenue of asking God may be the least exploited one. Many actually don't ask God for instructions simply because of little faith; they doubt whether God will actually answer them. The issue of little faith can manifest in many ways like asking God for what to do only when desperate. One thing that distinguishes asking from God from the other avenues is the kind of intimacy with God that it requires. A major impediment to this avenue is the failure to wait on Him for the answer.

We ask God for instructions by spreading the need before Him after believing that He can handle it or answer us first even before praying. Asking through prayer is an avenue that needs keenness and absolute patience. It brings about dialogue with God for you are dissecting an issue before Him, with Him, and not just to Him. It's not a unilateral deal but rather, a bilateral one. Both parties have obligations within the deal.

It's great to understand that God saved us through faith in Christ Jesus so that we, His children, can enforce His will upon the earth on His behalf. However, due to a poor spiritual foundation, many have ended up praying amiss or simply out of fleshly desires and emotiveness. Many end up asking for the little things instead of focusing on the bigger picture which is; God's will. It is the little children that ask their parents for temporary stuff, but grown ones desire to join their parents' businesses to work with them. This is the same concept with our heavenly Father who desires that His children eventually do crossover from childhood into adulthood. He desires that we may be performers, together with Him, in His Kingdom business.

Instructions are God's fundamental way of acknowledging how mature in His matters, His child is. How so? When God gives you an instruction, He brings along with it requisite provisions or all the relevant resources. Therefore, in other words, the person who receives instructions from God is a person that has been trusted with His divine resources. That person is now a custodian of God's provisions and there isn't a greater or nobler position than this.

Jesus Christ was and still is the Chief custodian of all of God's resources. This is why He states, without batting an eye lid, that *All things that the Father hath are mine John 16:15*. Jesus was given instructions by God to come and save us from the bondage of sin and death; thereafter, reconciling us with our Father. God gave Him power as a resource so that He would do His Father's will. Jesus received His instructions from God because He was trustworthy enough. If we look at how Jesus Christ managed His power and other resources that God gave unto Him, we will discover how instructions from God do prove that we are close to God. Many people are proud of having relatives in high positions; well, we have a relative in the highest office ever.

God needs His children to ask Him for what He is planning to do, so that they can be part of the implementation team. Co-workers have the same agenda with the management and are all in the loop. They have all agreed to work with a common mindset and agenda for the particular result. When you ask God for a car or job, He gives it to you from the position of a loving Father who is able to provide. However, when you ask Him for instructions, He relates to you as a partner. It means that you and He can now reason together, you can easily discuss matters and come to an agreement. It's only those that God trusts that He gives His instructions to and there is nothing better than God viewing you as a responsible child. Imagine God bragging about you to satan as He did Job?

Mathew 25:23 His lord said unto him, Well done, good and faithful servant; thou hast been faithful over a few things, I will make thee ruler over many things: enter thou into the joy of thy lord.

In the first verse, quoted in this chapter, though they were all in the same problematic state, we see David stepping away from the pack to get solutions for them all. He stands tall, above the rest by asking God for a directive on what he wanted to do which was to pursue the plunderers. Through this, God distinguished him from the rest, though they were all strong men. They later came to trust in David's God through David's receiving of those instructions. Men of faith ask for instructions because they know God's instructions will bring into force, the promises in the Bible.

Asking God for instructions is what proves to God that you are ready and mature enough to move into a higher realm of understanding. That you are now concerned with the major plans of God and not just the simple, little stuff.

20. FROM & THROUGH PARENTS

Proverbs 4:1-2 Hear, ye children, the instruction of a father, and attend to know understanding. For I give you good doctrine, forsake ye not my law.

Genesis 27:8 Now therefore, my son, obey my voice according to that which I command thee.

The issue of physical parentage goes beyond simple birthing and raising of children. Parents are tools of prophesy fulfillment. Even before we came into physical existence, God had already planned our very lives; where we shall be born, to whom and what our purpose will be. Parents aren't simply flesh and blood, they are God's appointed systems for our excellence and the fulfillment of His will. Everyone is a spirit and sprits need physical bodies and these can only be acquired in the womb of a mother.

Have you noticed how strong the devil's war against the relationship between children and parents has always been? It is so bad, such that there is the general belief within the society, that it is natural for teenagers to rebel against their parents. That it is a right of passage for everyone! These are carnal lies that the devil has set forth within the hearts and minds of men while backing up this lie up with numerous psychological explanations.

God never ordained that parents and their children be at war, regardless of whatever stages of growth that the children are in. This is because a good relationship with one's parents is the initial and evergreen source of instructions in one's life. It's the fundamental and original structure that our God did set in place for better living on earth. Of course this topic doesn't advocate that we should blatantly follow *unrighteous* instructions from our parents. It is only specific to the instructions that shall bring God all the glory. I do believe that you, the reader, is a person that fears God hence the choice to read this book.

God will never approve of heathen directives being carried out by a child even if it's under the parents' orders. God did specifically state, that everyone will pay for their own individual acts. A righteous son shall not pay for disobeying a wicked or sinful father's advice, he shall instead be commended of God. Even the laws of the land seek to find out the reason behind an action. A man cannot explain to any court that he killed in order to please his father. This is the same in the issues of God, don't disobey or displease God in order to please your parents. However, a lot of practical wisdom is also well required herein. We need wisdom to handle unbelieving parents who may decide to test our faith.

Jesus brought us into a new level in the area of taking instructions from parents. For thirty years, all the training and instructions He acquired were from His earthly parents and tutors. Things took a turn, the day the Holy Spirit came upon Him and God confirmed His Fatherhood over Him. Jesus was totally committed to God's will, such that He had to respectfully refuse to obey His mother when she desired to move Him from it. Please do note that He was respectful and not arrogant. Furthermore, it touched on His mandate from God. God's Word wonderfully overrules any other word.

Of course there is the fear of parental curses and that there are strong willed parents who never want to accept any other belief besides theirs. This fear is understandable but God knew this beforehand and made provision for it. This is why you cannot follow your parents' heathen systems when they ask you to. Note that it is when asked to sin. I know of a minister who was constantly sent to buy cigarettes by his unbelieving father. He thought that the son would one day prove to be disobedient due to the subject matter. However, through patient obedience over time, the father came to respect the son's Salvation and stopped sending him for cigarettes or smoking around him. May your timely obedience will make you a light to many around you. God will give you the relevant wisdom to handle the issue at the time.

The action of receiving the Holy Ghost means you are now a child of God and no longer subject to the wills of men; *John 1:12-13 But as many as received him, to them gave he power to become the sons of God, even to them that believe on his name: Which were born, not of blood, nor of the will of the flesh, nor of the will of man, but of God.* However, I should reiterate, that this doesn't mean that a Christian should go about disrespecting his earthly parents. Instead, it means, *"obey that which will bring you into God's favour but don't follow that which will make God angry."*

How can a Christian obey an alcoholic parent who instructs him to enjoy an alcoholic drink with him? How about a Christian obeying parental orders to pour libation to appease the spirits of the dead? This will be going against God's will. Jesus further demonstrated a powerful principle when He said that a person should deny himself and leave everything behind first in order to follow Him. He Himself fully practiced this. Loving anyone or anything else above Jesus makes you unworthy of Him and that's something none of us desires anyway. Your parents can help you build the best relationship with God.

> *Mark 10:29-30 And Jesus answered and said, Verily I say unto you, There is no man that hath left house, or brethren, or sisters, or father, or mother, or wife, or children, or lands, for my sake, and the gospel's, But he shall receive an hundredfold now in this time, houses, and brethren, and sisters, and mothers, and children, and lands, with persecutions; and in the world to come eternal life.*

My parents encouraged and urged me to serve God from a tender age and this is the best inheritance that I acquired from them. They created for me a good environment to serve God and to practice godly principles. I wouldn't mind if they didn't include me in their will, for a good walk with God is their greatest gift to me. It is the same thing that king David gave to king Solomon; the commandments of the Living God.

A godly parent's instruction is the primary source of God's favour. These kinds of instructions will bring you into the greatness that God has ordained for you. We notice how Jacob was blessed for obeying his parents' wishes unlike Esau who blatantly disobeyed. Obeying a godly parent brings blessings and disobeying an ungodly parent to please God, will also bring blessings. Godly parents produce fruits that please God unlike the ungodly parents who propagate or enhance the devil's will on earth even through their own children. Ungodly parents take their children, who are a gift from God, and teach them disobedience through various negative habits or vices. The first person to teach a child the fear of God isn't the Sunday school teacher but rather, that child's parents. Failure to do this leads to a spiritually stable family line.

> *Genesis 28:7-9 And that Jacob obeyed his father and his mother,*
> *and was gone to Padanaram; And Esau seeing that the daughters of*
> *Canaan pleased not Isaac his father; Then went Esau unto Ishmael,*
> *and took unto the wives which he had Mahalath the daughter of*
> *Ishmael Abraham's son, the sister of Nebajoth, to be his wife*

As I noted earlier, not all parents believe in our God. However, if your parents don't fear God, it's not for you to dismiss them, rather, it's your duty to bring them to God by shining His light upon them. They will see your distinction and understand that your God is truly God. it is good to understand that, even Mary, had to believe in Jesus Christ in order to enter the Kingdom of God though she hadn't believed Him to be the Messiah, at the start. The privilege of having the womb that carried His earthly form was of no use in her Salvation. She had to believe in Him as Lord which she later did getting her name written in the Book of Life. What if Jesus Christ had decided to obey her when she had ignorantly sent for Him, basing on her authority as His mother?

Long life on earth is vested in the obedience to instructions that a godly parent gives a child. God has vested much authority over children's lives in their parents. A parent can open or close the doors of prosperity in their children's lives. Careless parents are known to have derailed their children's lives such that life becomes a bitter pill for them. I have witnessed many peoples' lives go down the drain because of the altars that their parents built to tribal shrine gods. Some gave their children to their ancestors yet our God has decreed that the living should have nothing to do with the dead. Other parents simply make very wrong decisions causing anguish to their children.

> *Isaiah 8:19 And when they shall say unto you, Seek unto them that*
> *have familiar spirits, and unto wizards that peep, and that mutter:*
> *should not a people seek unto their God? for the living to the dead?*

Such a parent cannot issue life-giving instructions for that parent himself or herself is already outside of the will of God. There are people who have been forced to start brand new family trees because of the wicked family foundations that were laid by their parents. It will amaze you when you discover that most people today, suffer due to obedience to unholy instructions given by ungodly parents.

Dear reader, love *(agape)* your parents' and do follow their instructions but firstly make sure that they please God. God does and will always respect your parents' role over your life. If your birth parents aren't available, then your guardians or spiritual parents will play this role in your life. Always remember that God is the ultimate parent, even for our earthly parents belong to Him. He gave us to them as the fruit of their wombs, just as He gave them to their parents.

ABOUT THE AUTHOR

Pastor Erick Maosa is a minister of the Gospel of Christ Jesus. He is called to the Teacher's office and has a passion for building people up in the Word of God and in general life. He has been in active ministry for the past five years. He is also a public speaker who values the fulfillment of destiny in people's lives. He is also the youth pastor at Around the Globe Deliverance Ministry, serving God under the custody of apostle Francis Musili.